GRAND VALLEY UNIVERSITY LIBRARIES

AFRICAN WRITERS SERIES LIST
Founding editor · Chinua Achebe

Keys to Signs
* Short Stories
† Poetry
‡ Plays
§ Autobiography or Biography
Novels are unmarked

PETER ABRAHAMS
6 Mine Boy

CHINUA ACHEBE
1 Things Fall Apart
3 No Longer at Ease
16 Arrow of God
31 A Man of the People
100 Girls at War*
120 Beware Soul Brother†

TEWFIK AL-HAKIM
117 Fate of a Cockroach‡

T. M. ALUKO
11 One Man, One Matchet
30 One Man, One Wife
32 Kinsman and Foreman
70 Chief, the Honourable Minister
130 His Worshipful Majesty

ELECHI AMADI
25 The Concubine
44 The Great Ponds
140 Sunset in Biafra§

JARED ANGIRA
111 Silent Voices†

AYI KWEI ARMAH
43 The Beautyful Ones Are Not Yet Born

BEDIAKO ASARE
59 Rebel

KOFI AWOONOR
108 This Earth, My Brother

FRANCIS BEBEY
86 Agatha Moudio's Son

MONGO BETI
13 Mission to Kala
77 King Lazarus
88 The Poor Christ of Bomba

DENNIS BRUTUS
46 Letters to Martha†
115 A Simple Lust†

SYL CHENEY-COKER
126 Concerto for an Exile†

DRISS CHRAIBI
79 Heirs to the Past

J. P. CLARK
50 America, Their America§

WILLIAM CONTON
12 The African

BERNARD B. DADIÉ
87 Climbié

DANIACHEW
125 The Thirteenth Sun

MODIKWE DIKOBE
124 The Marabi Dance

MBELLA SONNE DIPOKO
57 Because of Women
82 A Few Nights and Days
107 Black and White in Love†

AMU DJOLETO
41 The Strange Man

CYPRIAN EKWENSI
2 Burning Grass
5 People of the City
19 Lokotown*
84 Beautiful Feathers
146 Jagua Nana

OLOUDAH EQUIANO
10 Equiano's Travels§

MALICK FALL
144 The Wound

NURUDDIN FARAH
80 From a Crooked Rib

MUGO GATHERU
20 Child of Two Worlds

BESSIE HEAD
101 Maru

LUIS BERNARDO HONWANA
60 We Killed Mangy-Dog*

SONALLAH IBRAHIM
95 The Smell of It*

OBOTUNDE IJIMERE
18 The Imprisonment of Obatala‡

AUBREY KACHINGWE
24 No Easy Task

CHEIKH HAMIDOU KANE
119 Ambiguous Adventure

KENNETH KAUNDA
4 Zambia Shall be Free§

ASARE KONADU
40 A Woman in her Prime
55 Ordained by the Oracle

DURO LADIPO
65 Three Yoruba Plays‡

ALEX LA GUMA
35 A Walk in the Night*
110 In the Fog of the Seasons' End

DORIS LESSING
131 The Grass is Singing

TABAN LO LIYONG
69 Fixions*
74 Eating Chiefs*
90 Frantz Fanon's Uneven Ribs†
116 Another Nigger Dead†

BONNIE LUBEGA
105 The Outcasts

YULISA AMADU MADDY
89 Obasai‡
137 No Past, No Present, No Future

NELSON MANDELA
123 No Easy Walk to Freedom§

RENÉ MARAN
135 Batouala

ALI A. MAZRUI
97 The Trial of Christopher Okigbo

TOM MBOYA
81 The Challenge of Nationhood§

S. O. MEZU
113 Behind the Rising Sun

HAM MUKASA
133 Apolo Kagwa Visits England

DOMINIC MULAISHO
98 The Tongue of the Dumb

JOHN MUNONYE
21 The Only Son
45 Obi
94 Oil Man of Obange
121 A Wreath for the Maidens

MEJA MWANGI
143 Kill Me Quick
145 Carcase for the Hounds

JAMES NGUGI (Ngugi Wa Thiong'o)
7 Weep Not Child
17 The River Between
36 A Grain of Wheat
51 The Black Hermit‡

AFRICAN WRITERS SERIES
141
Dead Roots

Arthur Nortje

DEAD ROOTS

poems

HEINEMANN
LONDON · IBADAN · NAIROBI

Heinemann Educational Books Ltd
48 Charles Street, London W1X 8AH
P.M.B. 5205 Ibadan · P.O. Box 45314 Nairobi · P.O. Box 3966 Lusaka
EDINBURGH MELBOURNE AUCKLAND TORONTO
HONG KONG SINGAPORE KUALA LUMPUR NEW DELHI

ISBN 0 435 90141 9

Printed in England by
Cox & Wyman Ltd
London, Fakenham and Reading

CONTENTS

ACKNOWLEDGEMENTS

'Preventive Detention' and 'At Lansdowne Bridge' were first published in *Sechaba*, the official organ of the African National Congress of South Africa. 'Thumbing a lift', 'Apartheid', 'Athol Fugard's Invitation', 'Continuation', 'Song for a Passport', 'Transition', 'Stream, Beach and Shadow: Scene', 'London Impressions', 'Joy Cry', 'Night Ferry', 'Waiting', 'Immigrant', 'Midnight', 'Windscape', 'Fading Light', 'Promise', 'Autopsy', 'Hiroshima 21 and the Lucky Dragon' were first published in *Seven South African Poets*, selected by Cosmo Pieterse (African Writers Series 64, Heinemann, London, 1971).

PUBLISHER'S NOTE

Many of the poems in this collection had been submitted to
Heinemann by the author, and were under consideration at the time
of his death. Subsequently, various additional poems were obtained
from various individuals after his death. Clearly, he was unable to see
the poems through the press himself, and he may have made
alterations and emendations had he been alive. He also sent many copies
of individual poems to his friends and to people that he met — some
of these texts vary and it is hard to tell which is the definitive version.
However, we have tried, with the help of the author's many friends,
to get as close to the author's intention as is possible in the
circumstances.

Thumbing a lift

Emaciated sand dunes and grease-black pylons
On afternoons teeming with impurities;
Brittle bitter-brown wire; the sky-blotching ravens
Must be September's electrified existences.

I live beside sap-fired willow striplings,
Yet alien to their cause, spring-exultation
Cars pass by the thin thing of my brown thumb
Rhythmically beckoning in painful indication.

Gnats swarm from scumcamps: above the asphalt
Shimmy-shaking witchdoctors gnarled like bluegums
Drunkenly perform their corrugated dazzle,
Leering through red heat with futile venom:

I scream in sad fury for movement home.
They ignore me, mama, they and their crazy
Machines, bright machines. Past this wheedling tramp
Cars swish and whizz in dust-whirling frenzy.

To be but a sliver of velocity pillioned,
Exquisitely frozen in foam-rubber pose;
Or dreamily sculptored in lavish freedom,
Trading vague pleasantries, parading poise . . .

There now, in chromium Chrysler Rambler
(Cream-leather atmosphere, cool man, relaxed)
Comes a smiling Samaritan – ah but those bulging
Ogres palm me off on an incredible next!

Trafficking with me now in truces of poison
White flags of exhaust fumes envelop my person
So I'm afterwards only O.K. when, chosen,
A cattle truck careers me towards the horizon.

South Africa, 1960–61

1

Midnight

Tonight, precisely at that wall
my room's floor pauses in its walk,
throws up a gaze, observes the clock.
Bulb and brandy begin to talk.

Energy flows and sounds emerge.
but not from me — some alien source.
Beyond glass panels at my door
the darkness grins with utter force.

It creaked, the room's one empty chair:
devil or angel on my seat?
Outside my window, lamps bead blood
down on a tired waiting street.

The toilet gurgles by my ear.
sucks someone's paper down the drain.
Its chain keeps keeping vigilance
on odours of bowels, odours of pain.

Night after night I lie and wait
for sleep's return, but she, but she
is gripped in spastic fists of fear,
trembling at noises made by me.

South Africa, 1961

Two women

Behind the counter, an on-the-prowl
Miss Modern. Strident high heels
rip, rip, rip at air or wood:
what is it to which she fails to kneel?

Perhaps men stud their floors with nails.
Ask her if you want to be impossible,
just don't get fresh, she'll wax sarcastic:
her conversations are confined to the till.

Coups you attempt from a distance
backfire — she forks your ego bar like a bone.
Hate her guts? No, sorry, that's up her alley;
she's strictly speaking a tigress on the phone.

Darkness should hone her sharpness then
when falling shutters signal her home.
But pounced on by night, isn't she rather
terrified by the stars, lampooned by the moon?

Cape Town, 1962

Synopsis

High white masses
of cloud delude me.
Wind floats, mingles
blue glimpses between.

Occasional rain
sings by green willows:
I watch the slant of
glittering strings.

Is the heart's country
all this loneliness?
Sundrops deliver
docile rainbows.

We've spoken. You
ignored the syllables.
Between the sentences
amass the silences.

Where have the men gone
who fought colour
theories, cracked spectrums —
back to the prisms?

South Africa, 1963

Soliloquy: South Africa

It seems me speaking all the lonely time,
whether of weather or death in winter,
or, as you expected and your eyes asked, love,
even to the gate where goodbye could flame it.
The last words that issue from the road
are next day regretted because meant so much.

All one attempts is talk in the absence
of others who spoke and vanished
without so much as an echo.
I have seen men with haunting voices
turned into ghosts by a piece of white paper
as if their eloquence had been black magic.

Because I have wanted so much, your you,
I have waited hours and tomorrows, dogged
and sometimes doggish but you often listened.
Something speaks on when something listens:
in a room a fly can be conversation,
or a moth which challenges light but suffers.

Should you break my heart open, revive the muscle
for March grows on with mounting horror:
how to be safe is our main worry.
To keep you happy I shall speak more,
though only in whispers of freedom
now that desire has become subversive.

The gulls are screaming. I speak out to sea.
Waters, reared for attack, break forward:
without a word, this violence. From the cliffs
above the warm, shark-breeding sea that drowns
the oracle of the vibrant air I walk
and hear the ropes that thrash against the flagpoles.

The wind's voice moans among willows.
Would you say that air can move so much?
It echoes so much of ourselves. In you
lies so much speech of mine buried
that for memory to be painless I must knife it.
it seems me speaking all the lonely time.

Cape Town, 1963

6

Preventive detention

Pale teaboy juggling cups and saucers
once taught Othello to our class,
and a spindly scholar's imprisoned because
winter is in the brilliant grass.

Liberal girl among magnolias born
was set to clipping dahlias
in the prison yard, her blonde locks shorn.
Winter is in the shining grass.

Twine the tattered strands together,
loves and passions that amass.
What's discoloured in the blowing clouds
winters in the luminous grass.

Cape Town, July 1963

Spell cold and ironic

Icy spell traps me after spring bred
fig's green rage, world's froth of blossom.
Cream burst to the surface, rain fed
milk and yellow lilies, I got
goldenrods where twigs had scraped some
warmth and moisture from winter's budget.

Streamers of colour in September's opulence;
water splashed laughs through my fingers, glistened,
danced my face in the element's brilliance.
Hatched eggs, flocks of new birds opened
freedom's country, offered the millions
blood's fresh chance to change and mingle.

But cold snap shuts one in at zero.
Before the switch could click the chill
wormed back into the bone's warm marrow
under half-grown feathers. Chill spell.
Meekness inherits one grime and cinders,
a host of yesterdays. But no tomorrows.

Ironcast sky: against the day I'll carry
something subversive, ash in satchel,
showing I've studied death's business, am very
prepared to report in heaven or hell
(barring of course a security leak)
that grey day gagged it – spring could not speak.

October 1963

Hangover

Dissatisfaction invites me nowhere
for even profit and loss discussion:
silence keeps me home, I'm lonely.
Lately escape became the fashion.

I am alone here now, here living
with shoals of fragments, a voice hoarse like rubble
shifted by currents.

'Bill is in for an infinite while
and that's why Tom went underground.'
But this is confidential
(better stick that poem away
before the Special boys raise hell).

After the pub, after blur in the vague room
wine carries me to sleep.
Groaning awake I ask for time and water.
Snores answer me and rats
clawing wallpapers with tiger paws.
No lice, luckily I'm a bastard.

What I possess is oddments mostly
picked up in O.K. Bazaars at cost price
(there I saw rich people hunt in the basement
or perhaps they were hiding).

My face in the basin after
gulping a goblet of aspirin
scared the mirror with subtle laughter
(I remember these bits and pieces blindly).
That day in a bungalow revolving events
through love and liquor
before your banning.
Supper at the Naaz, instant
coffee at nine, coming home tomorrow.

Raymond's Tretchikoff smashed from the bare wall
when Frenchie demonstrated football;
shebeens all shuttered made it worse,
Tom Dooley sleeping on his purse.

Turned into shadows and echoes, those whispers.
The sun has gone under the sunset,
the moon squats with a lonely pallor.

In case of foul play, imprisonment, death
by drinking (identity is
268430: KLEURLING
Pretoria register, male 1960)
inform Mrs Halford, Kromboom Road, Crawford,
house without garden. No reward.

October 1963

The same to you

Last time I made some love arrangements
they
materialised and no doubt I was
flattered if not flabbergasted.

She came beautifully
ruby-lipped and eyebrow-pencilled;
green she came and left
and brown dawn.
This, then, I said, is actually called
success.

The other evening to tell you of it,
clean and sober I came finally,
you rising in your casuals, saying:
Ooh Arthur excuse me, don't I look awful.

Maybe the call was unexpected.
I said nothing till you
came back ruby-lipped and —

Ooh excuse me Ivy I must
leave for some you know some
quick appointment. Honestly.
Later maybe yes will I come.

November 1963

Slip of a girl

lovely shadow thinned into distance
under the blow of strong light suffered
over the gnarled root draped and wasted
out of the thoughtstream how you trickle!

beautiful phantom by failed love fostered
elfin in willow woods: floating on summer
water our faces danced among ripples
slip of a girl on snap remembered

1963

At Lansdowne Bridge

After the whoosh of doors slid shut
at Lansdowne Bridge I swim in echoes.
Who fouled the wall O people?
FREE THE DETAINEES someone wrote there.

Black letters large as life stare you
hard by day in the black face;
above the kikuye grass to the sandflats
goes the boorish clang-clang of railways.

Darkness neutralizes the request
till dawn falls golden and sweet,
though a sudden truck by night
cornering, holds it in spidery light.

Cape Town, May 1964

12

Go back

That you were always sweet: untrue,
whether this break is clean or just
one of those blind fights between two.

No-one can claim that you were good throughout,
unless in tribute to a dead girl.
Wind turns the leaves about.

Rain gives the loosened leaves to the tides,
it is the wet season you can never bear.
And there is much that matters besides.

Being stronger I usually surrender:
with defeat the worst is, I think, over.
This time leaves me less willing.

Come under this sour light and see
your nails have burnt like acid.
I want to be free of fragments!

Second thoughts would have been sooner,
but brown roots of the grass survive
though verdancy is vanished from the footpath.

Because you are bent on suffering
until you die silent, therefore you must
go back alone. You came with me.

Cape Town, April 1964

13

Deliberation

Wine makes me lose her love
among new curves and hollows:
I slip the hold when crowded.
Sober and aware
her absence is acute:
I wrestle it alone.

She has no angles, contours,
or mathematical data:
and what image can so
haunt one: yes, with all of it in silence
she makes me her quiet companion.
The turn of day is gradual.

Cape Town, August 1964

Hamlet reminiscence

You too can't share your warmth and plenty
therefore my summer nights go empty.
Hot rains fill them with savage comfort.
Is love instinct, life's only hurt?

So then
creation
is minimum of words, huh, Ophelia?
I think of you, the woman, with shrill fury.

Cape Town, August 1964

14

Exception

The world can pass to whom it may,
violence shall strike when the need screams.
Who would gamble on his hunch, allow:
for each man's fancy I make room.

There are no people I can closely know.
When passion stirs the spirit
diffidence or apathy melts
the urge to make the joy deliberate.

Thought as I move unmoved:
endure the street's influence, the impact
of daylight, night within hours.
Between flows life through silence.

Only your eyes have pierced the stoic
defences of the undeceived,
and your arm's soft concern
transcends whatever else I have achieved.

South Africa, 1964

Act

Bleak times I breathe like this
face smothered in your shoulder.
And hair? Desire moistens
strands at the lips they live in.

Surrender disarranges
love into scented creases.
Your quiver muffles winter worlds,
I drink the warmth in silence.

You are what tenderness is left
and I so grasp with tendrils
that a bird cries secret eloquence
glides over the fleeting water.

Cape Town, 1964

Pornography: Campus

Singing sprinklers water the feelings
of grass, and how they shower April!
Southern Hemisphere's resplendent: the metal
nozzles ejaculate rainbows of crystal.

Sunlight, dizzy on the campus, spins
silver through raindrop trajectories.
In anticyclonic circumstances hills
stand silent in their cactus brassieres.

Valleys are empty like noon savannahs
but conquest of physical impulse difficult!
Rabelais in 80°F
would grunt disgust. And Baudelaire?

The mowing machines' sharp cruelty:
the fragments flew in the wide
breeze, leaping from the murderous edge,
the brown seed raped. Lascivious snarls

subdue the lawns. Continually life
is a hunt below the tousled surface
of pubic hair's blond shock, or jet:
we are bastards of debauchery!

Hands are blades of gold for prostitution
and eyes comb naked areas where clouds
bunch to suck the teats of blue peaks.
That ugly ending to The Grapes of Wrath!

South Africa, 1964

17

Separation

Wet day continues. The quieter wind
courts drooping willows while the light absconds.
Thrush song dissolves in the subtle
pulsation of waters. The darkness surrounds,

a black stance at a distance.
All life too the inner circle's apart,
further than I can reach at once
with the heart.

Separation seems all. I remember
your face so ringed with shadow
it hurt my every awareness.
Perplexed, I wipe the window.

Rain drones on and the bird sleeps
wordless. The thrush continues and the tree.
Only that inward poignance craves
nearness and meaning, totally lonely.

At no moment have I believed
that the long song's dead, though.
And I have often breathed the sweet
air, after rain, reminiscent of you.

Cape Town, 1964

Search

brandy orgy's aftermath
is spasm of guts, stagger and grab
the door: brown spew

I lie in ubiquitous darkness
my sour throat harsh with disgust
like many times before

we don't know the place and explore
the altered season's unusual days
the slow transition from the rose
bud to the bloom to the dropping bare

pool of lingerie: inarticulate
blue fumes linger
among your hair fallen, angel, over
your eyes

I love you i said to the ceiling
though limbs forget so soon
the moon

and the sea searches the shore,
wind panics the waves, you feel
spindrift sting the travelling air.
Tide retreats and there are the rocks, still there.

Hills and hollows are home for us
the rain-sigh over the valleys,
and we will never turn from these
ways to
unwind
        ourselves:
                I writhe

1964

Initial impulses abort:
that quick spark fades. The effort
consumes the warmth and forces beauty
into an alien mould.
Across the abyss the heart may be
but the link will never hold;
for often it's been found
that the heart is not a void
but barren ground
where roots have struggled and died.

Failure is not the heart's fault
have I heard it said by her
whose grace I much remember.
For once in my youth I felt
most fortunate to write
my love on her sheet of white.
And now, now who knows whether
because of her eyes and hair
a palimpsest is made
that puts me in the shade?

Port Elizabeth, May 1965

Windscape

Air-swept slopes of straining weed
plunge dimly to the dung-dry rocks,
shore cowers under the bilious sky.
The oil-scummed green sea heaves and slides
below my view from concrete heights
in struggle with the lurching wind.
Chopping into the curve the white surge
sprawls among boats in frothing nipples.

Sharp winds with venom flay
the brittle bones
or tug in ferocious gusts at clothes:
Rex Trueform suit from a summer shop
(what man about town, distinctive style?)
around my limbs the wool rags bloat.

Into the lull with movement treason
I stride braced like a rod, resistance sweet.
The lash bites back, a plane of grit
sheers up obliquely. Note
how eyes squint hard into destiny's balance.

Hug
walls and walk flat and
anticipate but don't look back
or spit in the sun's pale skimming face.

The street funnels flotsam; air floats, deceptive:
black wires dirge, then, take this door.
The wild slut howls for rain
to soothe her caked and aching hollows.

Port Elizabeth, 1965

Fading light

Over the hill under fading autumn
going vehicles catching light
dart feelers back to my stand of shadows.
Around my casuals gathers evening.

Violet deepens in these shallows.
Moths tattoo the pane, obtuse, and sharp
stars glitter with malevolence.

Mere night can menace innocence
hence memory of light persists.
The blaze of grass in our last green morning:
not garish, yet enough
to grip my careless glance.

That was once, and out of nature
I craved remembrance, light-suffused.
Conversation came between us, brilliant
grass and me in smooth June:
some bland response and you travelled
on, the price of petrol? And that was once.

Shall I now meditate upon the moon?
Twice bears no thinking. Experiments, seasons,
situations alter, but their instruments, tools,
equipment, apparatus remain the same:
the leaves, reversed by the wind, acknowledge
the wisdom of the wind.
I see how from all fissures reach
your features, spreading radiance.

Port Elizabeth, 1965

Bitter fragment

Of actual self each day, each word
exposes a bitter fragment,
erodes a grain of person;
and you can't justify
regrets or wistful longings:
time throbs within the heart,
all that we know is the bloodbeat.

Which eye can pierce the darkness,
which ear is cocked for silence?
Therefore you must endure
weatherings and exposures
as death is the final truth,
not malice and not love or magic spell.
Whose past is black or white no glance can tell.

South Africa, 1965

The long silence speaks
of deaths and removals.
Restrictions, losses
have strangled utterance.
How shall I now embrace your rhythms?

Dead issues, plans that failed
lie with our vanished stances
like stones in the windy townships.
Desires, once
brandished, have since
faded away like a bland murmur.

New developments
filter in
or even you with measured love
may break my tone of no response:
the loveless essence
remains the empty
nights and years, husks of the exile.

The soul has left
its slim volume
of acrid poems only.
Faint smoke is a sharper reminder
of fire and life than agile tongues.
Stench leaks from the gloomy tomb of treasure.

South Africa, 1965

24

Apartheid

Winter parades as a mannequin.
The early scene looks virgin.
We sway past in a Volkswagen.

Nothing outwardly grieves,
so luxuriant are the trees.
Leaf-rich boughs ride past with spring's ease.

Yes, there is beauty: you make
the understandable mistake.
But the sun doesn't shine for the sun's sake.

Flame-sharp, it beats casual
sweat from my aching skull
and the May winds are mechanical.

A bird's clean flight
exhibits the virtue of light.
I skulk in a backseat, darker than white.

How should I envy the luminous
sky if the cold and anonymous
men of the world strengthen my enemies?

It matters little that
this lane, this door is separate.
In the rare air have we met.

1965

Promise

Clock and season march, each day more mellow,
since time must nourish youth beyond the blossoms:
the new furred power glints in early patterns,
brought with true focus to your beauty now.

Words drift in multitudes from your replies,
who've chosen foreign life: I ponder snatches.
We crossed like shadows, young and watchful insects.
My time has turned to life beyond this room.

All loves have love-songs, once a girl well thought of
set spinning a lugubrious Italian.
You, mermaid with your criss-cross rain of pale
hair, never had favourites, just friends.

That sweet detachment lingers rich in influence.
O day beyond the curtain swarms and rhythms.
My song to you is imminent: sky and glittering
sea and the grass of quick surprise, our world.

The luminous air presents its gifts of fragrance,
myself with its first taste in flowering spring.
The wind strays off the water with desire
among these leafing boughs to fork me open.

As I grow outward, what has held me shut,
unconscious of your vigil, you my swan?
I am as strong and fluid as a river
to give your empty spring its first fulfilment.

South Africa, 1965

Athol Fugard's invitation

Yesterday an auburn beard
at a chance encounter, again after years
your keen eyes lucent, unafraid of fear.
Discussing the country we agreed to meet
to discuss the country over wine and curry
red and strong to give us courage.

Dawn glinted early, suffusing promise
of peace to palliate our common
brooding: there would be golden company.
Sun was the sequel above a smoke-
grey cloud but then the sun-wind rose
in wisps first out of the boomering bay
or rather it swelled to occasional
gusts and broke into livid gale!

Rain beats hard against the glass,
linen flaps on a drab balcony.
Boreas batters the walls — a windy conceit
because I lack the Nordic light
illumining a surface force.

Not that I spit of deceptive lustre
(I take it in my leather complexion)
or scorn the few redeeming features.
Around me squat the sombre ruins,
the charred hulks, the bizarre
wreckage of raids and deprivations.

And to give us hope?
No rare delightful image glistens
on cobbled multi-racial pavements.
White rain beats in stinging torrents,
vehicles pass in their earnest bee-lines.

1965

Continuation

Waking glazed into the murky dawn
and turning back into the dull body till it be day,
till it is summer or eternity:
deliberate postures hurt me.

Dim sloth aches. Numb muscles
express dumb mumbles, building
slow anger against a wall, but leave it:
brooding is deadly.
We found release in harsh liquids, bewildering.

Wry time ticks where stainless metal
nestles in ash on the stained piano.
Strange how
proud the limbs are, sprawled horizontal.

I am alone and isn't it love
to drain remains so the warmth steadily
edges along the blood, it is greedy for strength.
Love it is, lip-smudge on glass and the wine-beads
run back down the crystal. I now hear life:
alone in the room doesn't mean the whole house.

The hoarse voice searches. We compare
views of parties, find a need for food:
guts feel the acid pangs, I speak
out of passages hearing him bellow again at some staggering
        gaffe,
and continuation defeats
the bitter ascetic, despair; our words
starve that envious lusty glutton, the ego,
out of recognition: thus
we have long survived the stigma of being.

There are no more empty hollows. We
wake newly to find
sun and bird and leaf beyond in sequence:
our similar world, reassuring laughter
exploding again in an endless beginning
till it be echoed into eternity.

1965

The nimble razor smoothed the skin
gorging itself on lather scum.
The soap's round shoulders mollified
muscles that raged in the amorous night:
and in the new September tide
I gravitate to what is comely,
having tasted contumely
because my crust is black and hard.

In the mirror in the morning in a mood
melange such as one's swelling dream induces
I brief myself as you would were you near,
to whom my flesh was rainbow, heart was harsh.
Parting of ways exposed
love's tattered fabric
but the world rose
larger through the tears in bright enticement.

Who loves me so much not to let me go,
not to let me leave a land of problems?
O poet answer everything
so that the dull green voucher
can hold a shiny photograph
and miracles of destinations,
gold lettering endorsing many travels.

This world is grim and green, the houses
lie wrapped in mist from third-floor windows.
Glossy pages in the waiting-room feel
firm as leather and the print slides past.
Now interviews and checks are in the offing:
O ask me all but do not ask allegiance!

1965

Transition

Aqua-clear, the bracing sky,
and morning breathes cucumber cool,
invests the leaves with gentle airs.
My final spring grows beautiful.

Most lovely, not yet being lush,
athletic grace of limb and bud.
I stand self-empty, ascetic
in this my land of wealth and blood.

For your success, black residue,
I bear desire still, night thing!
Remain in the smoky summer long
though I be gone from green-flamed spring.

1965

Poem for a kitchen

Frigidaire resumes its steady throb;
drops trickle in ammonia's chill circuit.
Metal freezer furred with icicles
smokes zero cold the moment I lean in
to raid the stored glass bowl of plump tomatoes.
Magnetic fixture works the door by such
attraction as I notice leaves no vacuum.
Shiny enamel mirrors my drifting figure.

Stove's again a knobbed and dialled monster
with indicators, switches, thermostats —
and dizzy heat can curl from those electric
coils when once they redden — now all quiet
this squat chunk occupies the kitchen corner
invaded by the houseproud Mrs. Halford
with pumpkin fritter mixtures, apple sauces,
and other juicy dishes of the bourgeois.

What stillness settles round the gleaming Hotpoint.
Having disposed of human jetsam loads
its thick detergent scum has gurgled seaward:
filthy tides absorb the black remains.
And in my cool white shirt of Terylene,
my healthy socks that hug the feet in nylon,
and underwear that breathes through pores of freedom,
I smile sweet thanks towards the gleaming Hotpoint.

Built-in cupboards are edged with aluminium,
above which, polished, stands the breakfast toaster —
its plug has copper prongs split down the centre.
And crystal goblets glitter in the tray
across from dresser drawers which hold the silver.
To ban all cooking odours hangs there Kleenaire
(lavender). It titillates the nostrils.
The air itself, of course, is sterilized.

1965

Your absence

The moon be thanked for what
last night's surrender released
within her clasping limbs.
Numb in a morning body my bleak
find is a weary drizzle.
Life's ache throbs up from zero.

I flatter a casual
acquaintance sometimes.
Or entertain nubile
strangers completely
alone in this same

house where now pan's oil
ambushes albumen,
water strikes
icy aluminium.
The yolk quivers,
the leak's irreparable.

You would have opened
windows, touched
steamed mirrors.
Stood pensively musing
how many Rothmans and Stuyvesant stubs
it would take to fill one silver ashtray.

Sublunary illusion lacking
I slurp coffee
very realistically. Summer means
that days are long and in your absence searing.

1965

Casualty

Dust motes float through sunbeams in the golden
bitter that I sit and sip through slit lips.
The blue smoke that I blow is growing grey hair,
a spring ball poster flutters its pink flowers.
London is what I need in April
beyond the moaning distance of a girl.

Once we were together in the same country:
you were tiling out your heart already;
your father in the gold mine of his bedrooms,
the racket king of tenements. His ulcers
squirmed at the Sunday peaches. I have watched
him shyly stash his pockets with the black money.
My mother always hung upon the steam
of samp in soldered pots
and pumped the primus stove to drown my questions.

My devil is the bastard of desires:
outlaughing remembrances, he spits on the shards.
The brown lice are buried in old mattresses:
they smothered, feeding sweetly in my highways.
And the rats peeped from hiding when
the scissored bag had spilled me like a wombscrape.

Time is passing, I spin it from my finger:
Down from Oxford, I slice a scotch egg.
The budding sun of April throbs
softly in the city's solid muscles.

What mean your quiet sensitivities now?
That dark hue must suffer like a stain
in the pizza houses of Canada.
You haunt me with your graceful lady pains:
go flirt coyly with Winnipeg's popinjays!
Or shiver among fir trees with your tan thighs,
where dogs of the ice are snarling at their bitches:
may blizzards blast your sterile hollows!

I shall be true eternally towards
my father Jew, who forked the war-time virgins:
I shall die at war with women.
Let me roam in the earth's filthy miracle,
the fox-holes, the labyrinths
beyond man's reach of stars
or your swimming-pool of lovesongs, heart of title.

1965

Spring feeling

I

The changing light deposits dull
aching blood, the night's recall.
I drift through morning rubble,
butts and bottles, gritty memories.

In London's hemmed-in slender traceries
fuss the finches, spring-elated.
We need not lift the dawn curtain
to see the world surviving.

If I respond with effort
my brown boots in the grass crunch
the spring shoots in the damp meat of the earth.
If I stand and wonder,

nothing where I am
can make the soul not bleed:
the safety-first of cooler life
has wrapped your hands in cottonwool.

The mind is now a thoroughfare
for nudes and veiled emotions.
I must kick the poetry habit,
gold stains haunt my fingers.

II

The liquid of my look
that gathered on your buds
has melted from those flowers.
Clouds magnificently turn and bury the sun.

Posters in the pubs
announce the summer balls.
I am saying I am sorry
I spilled across your borders.

Chelsea, 1966

Cosmos in London

Leaning over the wall at Trafalgar Square
we watch the spray through sun-drenched eyes,
eyes that are gay as Yeats has it:
the day suggests a photograph.
Pigeons perch on our shoulders as we pose
against the backdrop of a placid embassy,
South Africa House, a monument of granite.
The seeds of peace are eaten from our brown palms.

My friend in drama, his beady black eyes
in the Tally Ho saloon at Kentish Town:
we are exchanging golden syllables
between ensembles. I break off to applaud
a bourgeois horn-man. A fellow in a yellow
shirt shows thumbs up: men are demonstrative.
While big-eyed girls with half-pints stand
our minds echo sonorities of elsewhere.

One time he did Macbeth
loping across like a beast in Bloemfontein
(Othello being banned along with Black Beauty).
The crowd cheered, they cheered also
the witches, ghosts: that moment you could feel
illiteracy drop off them like a scab.
O come back Africa! But tears may now
extinguish even the embers under the ash.

There was a man who broke stone
next to a man who whistled Bach.
The khaki thread of the music emerged
in little explosions from the wiry bodies.
Entranced by the counterpoint
the man in the helmet rubbed his jaw
with one blond hand, and with the other
pinned the blue sky up under his rifle.

Tobias should be in London. I could name
Brutus, Mandela, Lutuli — but that memory
disturbs the order of the song, and whose
tongue can stir in such a distant city?
The world informs her seasons, and she,
solid with a kind of grey security,
selects and shapes her own strong tendencies.
We are here, nameless, staring at ourselves.

It seems at times as if I am
this island's lover, and can sing her soul,
away from the stuporing wilderness where
I wanted the wind to terrify the leaves.
Peach aura of faces without recognition,
voices that blossom and die bring need for death.
The rat-toothed sea eats rock, and who escapes
a lover's quarrel will never rest his roots.

London, 1966

Stream, beach and shadow: scene

heavy, like snails, the pebbles seem to move
with a stone paleness of pain
downstream, reluctant towards the law
of gravity, the
                    bank under my buttocks
is root-firm, earth's earth, and unlike

green yeast of moss in shy
patches germinating to attention
when the sky is allover blue simply
and soft, i think

With the moon gone that was
at dawn a crescent of ash
I flick sunlight off my toes
                    and rise
among willow fragrances, leaves,
and the fellow-travelling shadow:
                              mute
little prisoner, the soul apologizes, how
you diminish or do you
                    fear separation? hearing

the gulls scream sad abandon banking
high above the silt mouth where the mothering
sea pushes wearily lapping up
the last gift of the land.

The tide drags weed, the sea's
sore knees breed my wandering
upshore along an elbow of sand to gather
shark's-purse, washed shells, sailor's baubles, driftwood
eaten smooth
          soul white, and bluebottles

hover about the massive tunnelling waste-pipes
rust-crusted. Knives cut bait,
reefer smokers cast their ragged lines,
a tramp breaks bread, squatting to watch:
they say the glaucous mackerel
                              bite best
there because manshit
                      has quality, is tasty

loosened roots of the bowels, though
rubber disposals are more poetic
floating gently, wombless and flat, in a rock pool

did i wonder why
                  sharks scuffle in the brown surf:
human limbs are the delicacies
                              a careless
swimmer makes first-class offal

but the zenith sun of summer
also delivers details round the substance
of blood bone hair and fang:
where I am standing dumb my slim
shadow is quiet as a bottom circle
dark, composed, unhaloed —
                          pared to trueness

1966

Hiroshima 21 and the lucky dragon

I am blameless as a bunny in the sights of a Texas sniper,
posing on lawns among the age's infirm.
Nurses stroll arm-in-arm with grave patients,
blonde in white uniforms. The air is fragrantly warm.
It is August, the era of football, the playboy summer.
In the National Shrine of the Immaculate Conception
Luci, the President's daughter, gets married, and meanwhile

Hiroshima comes of age; cool youths on Hondas
scatter the white pigeons in their path;
they are the fliers themselves, in leathers and denims.
The steel birds that shitted
mightily through the brilliant air
are junk on the scrap-heap of new generations:
the daughters radiant, silky as geishas. The late

incandescence of an unclear nuclear aura,
catching no echoes from the bomb of majority,
burned the Lucky Dragon into a coffin of white ash.
After its wandering on the clouded sea
the timbers probably rot
in some derelict dockyard of Japan.
No fish are wriggling in the glistening nets.
Moonlight on the wave is sterile.

The saki did nothing for their appetite.
Pus in their eyes, their scalps brittle,
the fishermen vomited blood wearily into the green spume.
The captain lies buried on the peaceful hill,
oblivious of the island's natural tremors.
I say happy birthday to the lingering victims,
dragged from my gaping chamber the morning
they suffered that prophylactic blast of atoms.

42

Removed, forgetful, we soon forgive
the gory orgy, whitewash the accident.
If I found a flattened city what could I do
but scream the lust for life?
If I lay in the ashes of my dreaming days
what could I do but wait for death,
untouchable in my radio-active sleep . . .

We shall survive to succumb in the megaton waves,
for now that the soul is a stone we can never be
safe enough to grant the ghosts recognition:
though we acknowledge with money and flowers
they stare us mute, the eyes appealing for passion.
Let them be nameless, those curt syllables
can never be memorable the way we are used to.

August 1966

Philosophy

Weakness is not your weakness, it is my
one chance only to establish contact,
to foster acquaintance with the hurt that's concealed.
A room, the underground, boutique
and your expression of modest absurdity
are circumstance enough to make
personable the baffled animal.

There are missing situations, chances lost
because of discipline or inhibition.
To obey books, to ridicule coexistence,
is the brittle procedure yielding no solution.
Between library shelves on an impulse
to harness the breathing silence I have
measured your eyes, brown as a cooked mushroom.

Half-parted lips, surprise; a mouth can die
going without taste or touch of value:
the still shape wafts me into awareness
needing an answer at least of tentative interest.
I love quiet colours, symmetry, a nature
sincere enough to turn a tense point
into an instant's amused acceptance.

Metaphors blossom in the blood-spoor of purge:
your frailties dissolve in articulate warmth.
When random dark descends on the blacked-out city
I voice my presence with conviction.
A man to be trapped in a lift with is
a snakecharmer bubbling with flute notes.
Thus lyrical, evocative I wish to be.

Let me describe the watercolour of meadows,
movement of leaves in relation to the moon,
the incandescence of dead quasars,
the primitive years of the ape evolving

the golden age of the pig. Your eyes are lustrous
apples of delight when we elude
the bewildering traffic, retreat to a ghost town.

And the night bears bouquets. The sequins of sound
I stitch on the garment of your heart are not
entirely self-inspired or rehearsed:
we agree in the jungle of life-time now
to cancel its tangles of purpose beyond
spontaneous recognition, the immediate
focus that sustains whatever weakens.

August 1966

For Sylvia Plath I

Hate for the father. A pool of malice in my blood
dribbles like yellowing water down that cliff-face of ferns.
His blood confuses mine, I do not forget
how age corrupts my clarity with snaking pain.
I lived with my girl's nerves calm on a plateau.
A man came with his love, I loved his vision
(the poisonous nest of words breeds visions) — he
was a younger father the way the superior voice
tugged like an undertow. Destiny said destroy them.

Flesh tears from flesh because it must
be acquired in a new amazing dominion,
assimilating the tyrant that bred it, to nurture
the conquering lord, who is handsome and stealthy, a boss cat!
I tried to pick the confetti seeds from my hair.
Night devours the marvellous colours, leans against the window,
the curtains rustle like stiff silk, the bedroom smells like a ward;
the scalpel glints of mirrors pierce my dark god
all I can feel is the burning together of limbs! . . .
The scorched surfaces refuse partition
till wind at warmdawn flimsies the poor and simple cinders.

It is another year, the summer
strangely evading my presence: can I befriend it?
I follow it under the trees, it recedes like a circle.
Evening gleam fades on the flowers, the moths are insane.
Rain scars the panes, the scratched message
conveys a stammered warning.
I read the scroll of the sky, it is grey with age yet young and alive.
Clouds shake their crystals out, white and beautiful.
I stand in a kitchen of poetry — scorch-black, cracked, and broken.
The soot sifts down to fill my channels,
perhaps to choke them, that would be more kindly

than silken tresses, as he called them,
sulking inside an iron chamber,
the green eyes glowing orange in the gas rings.

August 1966.

For Sylvia Plath II

Sensitive as a moon instrument. My
pen bites like a bullet. White and cringing
the paper bleeds black tears, it is inexplicable.
Yet all is wrought with care, down to the fine essentials
Practised, reliable, paying for truth in cash,
hands sensitive to the moon sinuously
lure the fluid from its channel. My hands are magnets
attractive in silence:
it is my mind that strikes and makes them assassins!

A high window is like a hole
of broken glass in the sky, the rifle muzzle
jaggedly glinting an instant to shatter the sun.
I saw the slug through a telescope
rip the seams of bone, the brain a jelly of blood,
the skull lolling on its hinges, glazed with overkill.

Venomous words are spat from the fire:
the wood of the heart splits, showing splinters
brilliantly. They cool into shards of the age.
This is our napalm year, the year of the million lost illusions.

Makers of steel and wheels, mail order merchants,
manufacturers of cameras, I acknowledge.
I admire our doings, yes, the shiny calyx
holding the platinum petals reports the desert:
transmitters bleep in the dry gardens of the moon.
The soul has been translated
by mystics, masochists, lovers, simple
sufferers, prophets of doom, and black comedians:
giving the age what the age requires, a purgative.

The light trembles with temporality.
I have touched it, getting my coat on:
light dances in my skull, there's a frightening lustre
I am donning my coat like a strumpet
to walk in the dark beyond a child's escalating cry;
he is scalded with flaming jelly
soon to resume his silence beyond the hell of blisters.
Guns boom below the forest of magnesium flares.
I stand at the edge of the clearing, in moon and shadow.

August 1966

Letter from Pretoria Central Prison

The bell wakes me at 6 in the pale spring dawn
with the familiar rumble of the guts negotiating
murky corridors that smell of bodies. My eyes
find salutary the insurgent light of distances.
Waterdrops rain crystal cold, my wet face in
ascent from an iron basin
greets its rifled shadow in the doorway.

They walk us to the workshop. I am eminent,
the blacksmith of the block; these active hours
fly like sparks in the furnace, I hammer metals
with zest letting the sweating muscles
forge a forgetfulness of worlds more magnetic.
The heart being at rest, life peaceable,
your words filter softly through my fibres.

Taken care of, in no way am I unhappy,
being changed to neutral. You must decide
today, tomorrow, bear responsibility,
take gaps in pavement crowds, refine ideas.
Our food we get on time. Most evenings
I read books, Jane Austen
for elegance, agreeableness (Persuasion).

Trees are green beyond the wall, leaves through the mesh
are cool in sunshine
among the monastic white flowers of spring that floats
prematurely across the exercise yard, a square
of the cleanest stone I have ever walked on.
Sentinels smoke in their boxes, the wisps
curling lovely through the barbed wire.

Also music and cinema, yesterday double feature.
At 4 p.m. it's back to the cell, don't laugh
to hear how accustomed one becomes. You spoke
of hospital treatment — I see the smart nurses

bringing you grapefruit and tea — good
luck to the troublesome kidney.
Sorry there's no more space. But date your reply.

August 1966

September poem

September tennis: a twang of racquets.
The sun is a gypsy among white frantic figures.
Balls lobbed and smashed volley their senses
but lose fur skimming the courts of my brain.

How I am disembodies as a cloud
though life is prickly as an autumn thistle.
Past does not cling, but spreads and settles
like colour in the water, heart's diffusion.

How unable to hear my own laughters
I hulk vacantly, nudging shadows.
Thought shapes, disssolves there where I view
fumes untwist from the domes of mown grass
Light, embalmed, recrudesces
brief and luminous on leaves that amber
into the dying season, spiders climb.
Rain suggests itself at nets and webs.

Tears are pointless, merely reassemble
deep ghosts in appropriate solitudes.
I, with my nomad loyalties, regardant,
find nothing to remember or prepare.

Trees already shed their seeds:
the windborne floats on loose, quite comely, air
to nestle against the imminent. Already
a wet cane chair drips lonely in the bottom of the garden.

Noticing time is a chance occasion –
the grubbier nails on my right hand
the neat split in a jacket's shoulder seam,
and these are details causing vague unease.

August 1966

51

Autopsy

I

My teachers are dead men. I was too young
to grasp their anxieties, too nominal an exile
to mount such intensities of song;
knowing only the blond
colossus vomits its indigestible
black stepchildren like autotoxins.

Who can endure the succubus?
She who had taught them proudness of tongue
drank an aphrodisiac, then swallowed
a purgative to justify the wrong.
Her iron-fisted orgre of a son
straddled the drug-blurred townships,
breathing hygienic blasts of justice.

Rooted bacteria had their numbers
swiftly reduced in the harsh sunlight of arc-lamps,
the arid atmosphere where jackboots scrape
like crackling electric, and tape recorders
ingest forced words like white corpuscles,
until the sterile quarantine of dungeons
enveloped them with piteous oblivion.

In the towns I've acquired
arrive the broken guerrillas, gaunt and cautious,
exit visas in their rifled pockets
and no more making like Marx
for the British Museum in the nineteenth century,
damned: the dark princes, burnt and offered
to the four winds, to the salt-eyed seas. To their earth
unreturnable.
        The world receives
them, Canada, England now that the laager
masters recline in a gold inertia

behind the arsenal of Sten guns. I
remember many, but especially one
almost poetic, so undeterrable.

II

He comes from knife-slashed landscapes:
I see him pounding in his youth across red sandfields
raising puffs of dust at his heels,
outclassing the geography of dongas
mapped by the ravenous thundery summers.
He glided down escarpments like the wind, until
pursued by banshee sirens
he made their wails the kernel of his eloquence,
turning for a time to irrigate
the stretches of our virgin minds.

Thus — sensitive precise
he stood with folded arms in a classroom
surveying a sea of galvanised roofs,
transfixed as a chessman, only
with deep inside his lyric brooding,
the flame-soft bitterness of love that recrudesces;
O fatal loveliness of the land
seduced the laager masters to disown us.

36,000 feet above the Atlantic
I heard an account of how they had shot
a running man in the stomach. But what isn't told
is how a warder kicked the stitches open
on a little-known island prison which used to be
a guano rock in a sea of diamond blue.

Over the phone in a London suburb he sounds
grave and patient — the years have stilled him:
the voice in a dawn of ash, moon-steady,

is wary of sunshine which has always been
more diagnostic than remedial.

The early sharpness passed beyond to noon
that melted brightly into shards of dusk.
The luminous tongue in the black world
has infinite possibilities no longer.

September 1966

Chelsea picture

Dim among mists a starfish floats, the sun
of London autumn, leaves with everything.
The wind has found its orphans nooks,
though some, soft with the weight of rain, are trodden
pulpy in the concrete of embankment.
I scan a lacing shower pearl the water.

Occasional surprise, that gold eye's blinking:
acutely comes the light off surfaces.
One would have thought the moon the more capricious,
but nightscapes lack such clear diplomacy.
In the King's Road Sunday traffic
pursue their reasonable functions.

Cold of an unknown purity cannot swear
a man from tropical Africa in more firmly:
crisp to the soul air's essence filters,
my hushed breath wreathes affirming tacit answers.
Rain, as I find, is not at all perpetual.
What other introduction one expected!

London, 1966

London Impressions

I

Out of the Whitehall shadows I pass
into a blaze of sun as sudden as fountains.
Between the bronze paws of a lion
a beatnik stretches his slack indifferent muscles.

Nelson's patina of pigeon shit
hardly oppresses that plucky sailor. Cloudbanks
lazily roll in the blue heavens beyond.
The birds home in on seas of seed.

Foil tins float on the dusty water.
The walls are full of faces and thighs.
I smoke a Gold Leaf close to the filter,
viewing dimly the circles of traffic.

The isle is full of Foreign Noises
that jangle in trafalgar square,
England expects every tourist
to do his duty now the Pound is sickly.

II

A girl plays games with mirrors
in Hyde Park while I'm half-suggestive
with the dolly scanning a volume idly.
In the flare of an instant it takes to light
a cigarette:
against her treetrunk comes to lean
the ugliest bloke that you have ever seen.
Predictably they disappear
through the distance of August green.

The nymph on the grass behind
proves her point by blinding my return look.
She picks her black bag up and drifts on further,
not helpful as to whether I should follow.
Meanwhile a huge Alsatian sniffs my loose boots,
the gentleman with the leash exchanges gossip.

Sun, you are all I have:
the grass already welcomes the brown leaves.
I do not want to cross the road again,
having learnt the value of other faces,
acquired the pace and tone of other voices.

And big red buses; I thought I would never catch
sight of the gentle monsters
when I was young and shackled for my sharpness
in the Union of South Africa.

1966

Collage of The Times

While light crawls in to find the birds alert
the times have been but fodder to our dreams.
What's Hecuba until the sleeper wakes?

I hear the world's news plopping on the mat,
the milk cart rattles by in London grey.
I upset the candlewick creases, stirring the warmth away.

Towards my shoes I yawn, impossible cry,
having decided to write poetry
from memories like small ads on the front page.

Monday of Easter, His Ghost must rise, besides
the marriage of Figaro, death of a Salesman:
all (per line) for twelve bob, box numbers extra.

O world of sport — battles in mud, dramatic finishes,
what happens to the Test if rain clouds picture.
Results at a glance show I've lost some money.

What the Prime Minister said on Oil
jostles the views on abortion reform,
homosexual control, drug legislation, etc.

And how well have they worn, the loved ones?
Certainly our enemies became companions.
Mr. Jitsu Karate joked with us nostalgically.

Under a brilliant sky the hatches opened
to shit their nuclear droppings on two cities.
Since then I loved the bomb, there is always a first time.

Easter uprisings and safari rallies
have made the back pages. — Once in Africa
the pink flamingos ignored the Mau Mau rumours.

And south of the border there has never been
a sanity of purpose in the laager.
God's stepchild cannot be their son-in-law.

1966

Period

Boredom rather than moony booze
should crown my nights neutrally
beyond the reach of harlots or divorcees
rasping in my pockets for milk money.

The abandon of wine scuttles priorities.
I swagger like a sailor from the stale sea.
Lean and raucous I thrust my stubble
among the birds that clamour on the quay.

If aftermaths ensure, it's you I choose, but
alone, I can be tough, not needing guts
to pamper kids who find me naked and sleepy.
And no curtains stay squalidly shut,

love's grim burlesque. Yet this remains
reality. Your kisses cling
like peach-halves to my scrofulous kernel.
I find your garden's roses bleed in spring.

Your smile tells my half-happiness. The moon
lampoons desire, shines with gelid ripeness.
You lie in your bed of thorns
your fingers casually piteous.

September 1966

Assessment

But one the adventuring survives,
with phantasmal ease, despite
sick teeth that loosen in their gums
and the palate of morning-after autumn.
I wake clammy from a dream
with eyes that cannot focus on the keyholes,
and the dark is clasping me in soiled sheets.

The survivor walks away
through the gate, the street of leaves,
with dry footsteps. My feet slither
after the wraith wearing parts
he has carved away from this other half.

Baffled, saddened, I maunder, returning
among the fallen corpses. He
cannot come back.

Oxford, October 1966

Affinity TO MAGGIE

my blood mother mourned
the damp and gloomy evenings of our country
whose womb hurt with deadweight

my seeds have fallen in absences
sunlight dried them like
spittle on asphalt

lack of belonging was the root of hurt
the quick child, he must travel

new views of greening trees alert
my sensitivities and why
should I deny them

my eyes lit up and answered
to your sweet timidities
I love your

reticences

Oxford, 1966

Newcombe at the Croydon Gallery

The dealer in shirt-sleeves told his assistant Jenny
to serve champagne to a tall supercilious lady.
Middle-aged Americans in sneakers,
peering closely, noses to the gouaches,
jostled the dainty natives, and a Rolling
Stone in executive grey arrived
without a murmur among the objets d'art.
Upstairs against the ebony panels
under the chromium lamps a woman stood
deciding to buy Bill Newcombe's watercolour.

A small posh opening in the arcade
with suave young professionals, he the self-taught
veteran shown in Paris,
Sydney, Moscow, San Francisco, New York,
props himself on his stiff leg, looking bland,
back now, still in exile, on an island.
Across the strait, with a view of Vancouver
he built sand castles, trapped birds in his boyhood,
cut timber before the war, started creating
those weird spindly shapes which sang
the lyric of the standing birch along the pulsing blood,
peeled lean and white.
                          The Royal Air Force
claimed for a space of time his gift.

Hence experience is learning:
no violent punctures, interrogation rooms,
surrealistic phalluses or soup tins inspire him.
There are no birds, guitars, or flowerpots.
His flimsy tumbling squares
seek each other at normal moments
where line and tint converge,
the anguish being level with the eye,
yet not concealing any of the gaiety.

Tonight the private view goes on too long:
he grumbles sceptically, blames his Welsh wife.
Nervy, she shakes her rosé,
offering me a cigarette.

From an iron pit close to the twinkling stars
he peeped tinily into a hell of flak,
the lights bouncing between long stretches of dark.
Or he tattooed the visible sky with smokeplumes
cooped in the belly of a steel dog
till shrapnel studded his ribs with scarlet jewels.
But it is twenty years later or so that I hear
the story in bits and pieces.
We are drinking Spanish sauternes
in the top flat of a brick house, Highgate, London,
and winter returns to the landing:
the owls hoot at night.

Now that I travel away I remember
the soft greys of autumn, the ambers of autumn,
the quickness of seasons, occasions that change,
the din that rises from the lobby where
a Pakistani in a dressing-gown
natters over the telephone,
and our wine-rich laughter while
over the cold fields the thick air settles.

In retrospect appears his face
complete with puckish wrinkles
underwritten by the grey goatee:
though I have also seen at dusk
thin leaf-blades of his eyes observe austerely
the feeble warmth that now is alone available.
To survive, may he have meant,
one must choose the possible.

Oxford, December 1966

64

Winter: Oxford

I

Winter in a mini-skirt, thin-faced, will come
in white boots up the thirteen bleak
steps to the door of the Radcliffe Camera.
The pinnacles lose their honey colour
recorded by a million tourist lenses,
and water drips through the canvas rigging while
a man hidden in the scaffolding calls
above the green ripple of grass for a rope and a bucket.
The old stone dies, and nothing is restored.

By the river the raw nerves wince
where wind bends into the trees:
west is a grey afternoon beyond
wet silhouettes of traceries. The grey
current carries the surrendered leaves.
Leaf-blown lanes where tendrils wither
in brittle crevices are paths I take. Now
barren rags motley the gardens,
their brief lives half-remembered. Lonely
with an ungloved hand I smoke.

Birds are occasional. Swans
nestle with inscrutable melancholy upstream.
A bridge arching low shelters
reeds that imprison flotsam.
Punts at rest knock softly,
emptied by our May nights.
Cobwebs lift and flutter in eddies.
The boathouse smells of the ale of summer
now stale, I note with sympathy.

II

In the warmth of the college cellar
where the thick steam pipes exude

the comfort I hunger for, I feel
droplets of sweat cold in my armpits
easing through the thin dew of deodorant.

Ribs in the age of pornography are
swathed in fat as thick as several
rolls of soft pink toilet paper.
Bleakly I smile at graffiti.
The haemorrhoidal itch gets me.

Summer was good value:
I came like water and like wind I went. And now
I suffer reduction to an ineluctable
purity. A biggie plops
in the water that leaps and stings.

III

I am forced upon austerities: the soul
glimmers feebly in its bed of pork.
Lights go out in the hospital,
the blue glow is only the night lamp.
The world that I move in knows
no sheltered pleasure. Alone I have seen
gutterwater bear away white petals.
My grubby mac dripped English rain.

You, chill-faced winter, follow leering along
the trail of gobs that weigh my cobwebs down.
On porcelain thrones of cubicles I've sat
to think away an exile long impoverished.
Who can pay for my safety now,
and why is it so ineffable?

Oxford, December 1966

Americans in town

Sitting in late
        light with acquired faces
my tongue breeds blood desires, picks the weight
of necessary detail from some instances and cases.
Sly like wine I snake along the veins,
though not without some truth, the vital grains.

A girl's laugh can
        turn my gaze to her symmetries,
and even the ugliest glamorous wealthy American
is seen in passing to be amazing; these eyes
dance under smoke-black beams of an equable
pub where beer ringlets shine on the table.

Gay answers ring
        through the green life of trees and grey stone.
Or puzzlement creases their faces, or something
elicits smiles when they have grown
less watchful and mortal under my care: which one
to single out and offer my attention?

The deeper I
        look the more there's poignancy, and
it leaves me tender at the heart, so let me lay
muscle along muscle, shut the mind.
Relinquishing the vortex of a glass
with bruised lips I print my wishes.

They all travel
        through summer having roused that latent blackmail
of sun that dazzles, blue-gold days, and still
I spin the blind web, waiting with a smile
as if the weather of life is always good
and my nights were never dead ordinary, dead.

D

It's what I like
          now, my life, the world of birds, dusk, sequence
without result, but purpose that can strike
to bend her will at any moment. Once
I thought of love as permanent, but since
I've come to know the growing grey of absence . . .

Oxford, 1966

The Near-mad

Faces gather in rooms with stony features:
eyes that glimpse you coldly, breath of ozone.
Rooms are full of airy delusions:
oh how they have crumbled the heart's empire!

They haunt you to lunacy, the cool receptions
of letter-writers, their empty statements.
You thought she loved you but where is the evidence?
Anchors have snapped and roots are severed.

Optical assaults have terribly shrivelled
the tendrils of feeling. The tyranny of wheels
has left you immobile in countless vehicles.
You have been drunk at parties, slept with peach blondes.

Or smoked hashish, swallowed the lights, speechless,
your belly hollow with bulbs and neon tubes,
feet floating across the path. You discovered too
the tension for action that eats like acid.

Midnight over the phosphorescent sea.
Back at the hotel hard bodies bob on the dance floor.
You lie like an assassin in wait for the moon:
but your jugular swells, your wrists can stain razors.

The chilling immensity of wet dusk
descends invincibly upon the city.
Under the skin into infinity
scream the alcoholic blood, the blurred tissue, the crazed muscles.

The anxiety exists that desire no longer
directly affects the once simple interiors.
A hair's-breadth from the edge of hell
you hug the miracle of dreamless sleep.

On lidded eyes impinge the facts of daylight.
Nortje, your face spilt hairdrops in the mirror
yesterday. You are to carry
a black umbrella in the rain from now on.

Oxford, January 1967

70

To John, Paul, George and Ringo

The simpler impulse living in a girl
finds harmonies across their microphones:
there is no money that can buy them love.
The mockery endures, being magnanimous.

Doubts of the heart can vanish in a song
that rises again to the lips like instinct.
These cameos of melody, that acute
lyric, a guitar wail, nuance — voice me.

The light I have lamented, poems lost
in half-sleep between the day and the last dark,
my epitaphs for people, elegies, odes
are but the deeper breathing of an age.

You, wry John Lennon, the pretty imp McCartney,
Harrison the taciturn, gothic-featured Starkey:
the new gospel's four phenomena, they
themselves would laugh at the terminology.

In the network of hair mischievous smiles
revolve, that help to pass a hard day:
the warm burr with its edge of truth
strikes many exuberant affinities.

Reluctant idols of the country, Liverpool's
gift to the jaded south, intellectual targets,
and export fodder (medals from the Queen):
a chord falls oddly, a voice trails, rhythms startle.

Sometimes rubber-souled, but often moving
in the further places beyond words,
having no message but the music native
to our time and mood — they enliven the minutes.

January 1967

Discopoem

In the middle of my fix i think
we are all together, a mexican a japanese
a dolly in a discotheque and mona lisa
and president johnson and engelbert humperdinck.

The grateful dead at a california weirdo
brought out their crackle gear, trailed microphones;
the audience was wild on banana peels
and sent an usher to buy some grass for two

gurus who had fainted on the joss-sticks
smoking, impaled on a phallus in the passage.
The chairman read The Medium Is the Message
which the inner few investors of Northern Kicks

kicked off their shoes in the boardroom to
the strangled jangle of the intercom.
One baron, delighted, name of Blom,
switched on his walkie-talkie, with his new

cravat in Warhol floral mopped his brow,
spoke to the boys at the Group Research Plant
behind the Church of the Happening Saint:
had they checked the Xerox talent-multiplier, the Now —

Machine, tested the temperature of
Thigh Acres and those vast suburbs?
An A and R man was writing the blurbs
for Mickey and Dozy, the Pooh, and the Much-in-Love.

The guest stars, the star guitarists, guitar
tuners, the players of electric organs,
The Mellow Yellow people, the Gorgon-
Zola Eaters were there or were not there.

April 1967

72

My mother was a woman

Your child is born with its soft skull:
I see the cord to be severed through
the microscope of my bewildered eye.
The growth shaped, muscle-spilt, is going to

its foster home: your young cave, void, relaxes.
Come thighing into May Day, watch the light
glitter in the water by the bridge where punts
float downstream with their classic smooth-limbed freight.

You will find me in a dead-end under bough-shade. You seek
momentum now the pageant has dispersed.
Is yours the president's message, is it a virtuous
philosophy offered the heroes in their hearses?

There are those who are irretrievable. I can think
of the Soviet colonel plummeting to hell
in virgin forest, no-one there, three trainees
burnt to cinders in a Florida oxygen cell.

You came from the German miracle and passed
rubbery through my life leaving the floor
littered with dollars. You pocketed poems, left
for Boston with my imprint on your decor.

Do you have thoughts of Dallas?
I promised in the night spent making love
you could pick me up by helicopter.
There are those who hope, like me, not to arrive.

Something dies when something else appears:
The milk that cannot permeate the blue
steel existence, quietly in the glass
syringe affords me some drab ecstasy.

We study needles, merge them with the blood
at ninety in the Mustang turnpike. Poet
is up in the sky with you and we are laughing
on a seismograph that's steady and cool, like heartbeat.

What other indicators, evidence,
of love and of identity do we need?
They are importing the exotic narcotic,
sugar from Cuba, Indian hemp and seed

of poppy, and the grey world should be grateful.
These make you remember ruined peoples
and make you forget that your teeth are rotting.
There are things that will wreck us, things that will help us.

Being now in earnest, I will find you are
always going to be the same — the yester-
children you flushed down to the Pacific
will never help to avert a third disaster.

I came to England, learning as was taught me
the message of your eyes, hair's golden rain.
From Cabo de Tormentoso I was hounded:
the salt in my flesh clouded my bones with pain.

But wherever I am going to settle,
whether in her arms at Saskatoon,
or at a London bus stop, waiting patiently,
it will be under the blood-curse of the moon.

May 1967

Identity

Infinities of images clash in my mirrors,
The fashionable urges that turn out to be
sterile, complacent as the moon in June.
Miscellaneous notions violate me.

Familiar gesture in the gents
at Paddington Station: The wristy aesthete
in pinstripe trousers, pale lizard, beckoned:
porcelain tiles reflected me vaguely declining.

Can I speak of probity, who now
work for the garbage man, stuffing the bin
full of tissue paper, sugar packets, anything
on which a poem was ever written?

Brushing promiscuously past with pointed
ears like a rodent and eyes that are casually dead,
a man with twenty watches on his forearm
flicks his sleeve down to the shake of my head.

Soft as a pig's heart muscle in a queue
down the Edgware Road, or in Leicester Square,
a revealing smile was prelude to a
supple suggestion, i.e. room to shave.

Do not interpret this only, the odd
encounters, the sought liaisons. See me
tickled at the bourgeois games on Saturdays
in pet shops, rows of Fido foods, canary

protein, whiskers cat meat with the message
Was it me eating horse in 1916
in the first great universal terror,
or dealing out poison chocolates at Belsen?

What indefinable blemish lets remembrance
now focus on a scar an intimate wrinkle?
The dead poets of Europe, the non-poets of the Soviet,
the poets of war of Vietnam: none can tell me.

May 1967

Song

Pain needles me to sing
where love exists in finitude.
Affection's swansong is anguishing:
a lyrical miracle your lips that bleed.

That smile once altered me,
my dark within, the glow of flame that was
your voice at now and then times. Then the pearls
fell through your grass.

The symmetries that satisfied
the light of dusk discolours.
I burrowed through your navel, issued
by convolution at your ear.

Ask me recompense, I cannot pay,
cannot redeem the promises I pawned.
Has the luggage that I lost not
turned up in the office of your mind?

You will find my journal, you may work
the memoirs over. The scope
you give the story is how it must ever travel.
You have soft hands, you were hope.

May 1967

Message from an LSD eater

An acute vacuum is imminent
when grass has withered over the cold fields
after continuum of anxiety.
Who has taken a fortunate trip
beyond the moon, past violet stars, through luminous soundwaves
invisibly travelling the years' kaleidoscope
falls back into the sea of capture,
is earthbound, banal, nauseous, sorry.
The observer of time is briefed by clocks and dates
gearing himself to certain numerals
Roman or Arabic. Death deliver me.

It is the circular anguish-making motion
that fascinates sometimes. The thin red needle
which never points anywhere is thus predictable.
This level of activity the eye can cope with
in fact if I cover
the traces of heresy. Eat the evidence.

However, a pinpoint can magnify:
the centre of tension expands tremendously,
silence ticks with a velvet hammering,
impulse ache. The soul dangles
like a butterfly mashed against a stainless flywheel.
It is depth that inevitably hurts, and regrettably
one must be broken open to find
it is the relationship that fails as therapy:
the heart's worn cogs, the mind's snapped links.

Surface diseases have diagnosible symptoms:
you can identify the features of a peach,
but teeth have animal urges
going deeper they bite the worm
and once I touch you it's not so simple
to discard the residual image

of marmalade on sick pudenda.
The throat burns.
The vein of a figleaf exudes milk.

A light hangs in the mirror by its frayed cord.
Cameras come between us to record it.
I am distracted by movements and jagged voices,
attack is from the air.
I go down the manhole of self-thought
testing the stench of tunnels. You
are nevertheless my favourite pterodactyl.

The final and sad wish is to be
absolved from apocalyptic questions.
Phoenixes are mythical, but is a tomato
fruit or what? Is a virus vorpal?
Solutions are latent in a cube of sugar:
sweets for the acid at any time
and anywhere must be a pleasure
amazing in a world of kidney machines.

When the bowels sigh in passing and it is night
the ghost on the landing desires
a glance at the notes I intended to send
from underground urinals and airport buildings.
Who can distinguish
the dialogue from the graffiti?

I am unsettled by a ghostly snore,
being buried in mud, life-locked.

England, 1967

Episodes with unusables

I

At dawn I rise to water.
Smelling the stucco and my shoes, leaning
into a wisp of air through shafted sunbeams:
it is another relief to be alone.

My liquid drops ammonia jewels
smoking in a net of grass.
Such a brief while the art of scintillation
lives in a miniature rainbow, the spring
earth tells me that all my words now,
my winter phrases, my wrought sentences
are dead as the thin conversation of evenings.

II

Tomatoes sprout in the garden, green
lettuce, the cool potatoes of the earth:
seeds we had thrown there, through the window,
through the door, where you
stood ready to make love, guarding my movements,
accepting my muscles, and I was thinking
how we were two, meshed in a kind of tenacity.

We have not watched
the sun shrivel the skin and eating
the juice of the unusable.
We have been locked in sleep, you have been fearing
the third growth, the fruit of nature.
I have groped in the rubbery darkness,
your cry has shattered all my integuments,
the total ecstasy has laid me waste.

I have loved you. We have not seen
the patience of waiting the seeds suffered,
the weathers they withstood in their infinite wisdom,
the tiny roots that felt their way into life,
the tendrils that clung.
Your hair fell over my eyes,
your aching beauty held me rooted.

Oxford, 1967

Exposure

You carry news from distances to
people in the home town who enquire.
Macpherson with a forkful of spaghetti
eyes you as an ornament whose coolness
could suit his living-room. An old professor
yearns to pinch your behind. Young businessmen
taking tea with your father are distracted.
They make bad bargains. At the ball
you danced with style. Only I see
your face is scarred with secrets
from localities of flesh, the burns and wounds.

Unanswerable, my questions grieve the darkness,
thought upon thought that crowds out sympathy.
Up the unclimbable side I have scaled
that mountain standing in the wintry straits.
They should have built a lighthouse on the ledge
where I bivouacked a night or two.
At the top there is nothing
but a hole that leads back into the bowels.
The first climber perished in that abyss:
the pitons have been rusting in your thighs.

Your dawn hair is disshevelled after midnight.
Make up your mind and cry;
cry to the city, the hard walls, whoever wants
the details of the cocktail party.
They have opened your skull with cutlery
from the coffee-table.
With a toothpick your mother
fishes in her bourgeois world, your sister
hustles you into confessions.

They want your life. The unborn
children need your life. My knowledge is
a tale of disillusion merely,

a parody of self in shattered mirrors.
I notice gaps wherever we have spent
time in the grass together;
scalp and bleak knuckles.

London, July 1967

Conversation at Mathilda's

Tea from the china pot in your afternoon
includes the rain along one window
my hand that trembles wanly
exploring the warmth that seeps into the flesh.

Veils drift over the mountains:
their faces and backs are forested.
The rain seethes with eyes over the river:
it is a strong and silent grey colour.

Intent on cutting through. There are leaves
wrenched by violence from their summer nodes
that merely float now into the lower world
passing with apathy through one more movement.

You will not be amorphous. I can gather,
soaking the puddle on the sill with a towel
and leaving it there for the duration of the dialogue.
Your thoughts reach back to Cape Breton Island's

lobster and cognac, father who is another
woman's companion, sister who is a nun:
no known loneliness that rain can foster
is ever going to bury sundown it seems.

Yesterday I wouldn't listen further
to my soul pulsing, turned in the street
to cash a cheque, read in my room a letter
from Ottawa, spent the day on my feet,

thought I couldn't afford another poem
in terms of time and breakage through the surface
which has to be patched together on a Monday
when there are no more arrows in the quiver.

There is no tomorrow which hurts me
after all preparations, only there is
the lacerating ritual of this minute
that I'm bleeding in the television age.

Voice them again, your voluble words,
there is virtue in the active chemical.
I exist between you and the world
like a catalyst, my ear designed for all

expressions of courage, love and disenchantment.
So I stood in the laboratory of the mind,
weighing moments, waiting to write up results
while you articulated the apparatus.

British Columbia, September 1967

Worded thing

Stranger in the glassed air that you meet
with this word world and this thing life.
Could be a brittle fancy as you stand
smoking a cigarette in the fall garden. Knife

a leaf idly, extending a mortal muscle,
being the boss of your own imagination.
At the base of your spine the puckered balls
sympathise with a plum in the grass that is worm-eaten.

Storm of time is the old dimension
you of choice choose to be out of now.
The relative reality is a flower,
and what of the sounds we are not attuned to,

the sonic system of the bat, the rat's
adaptable manners that enable
accompaniment to the arctic, to the moon.
All things flow or are escalatable.

British Columbia, 1967

Joy cry

Apollo's man-breasts smooth and gold-blond
hold between in the fine-boned cleft
the kernel of radiant light. Like wind
youth's madness streams through orifices. The swift
vivacious morning shoots along the ripples:
in my loins the swelling pearl moves.

This growing jewel wants to burst
through coils and meshes the seasons have wrought.
That time can tame the green surge,
that age can quell the riotous blood,
my eyes, blind with their glory, shun.
The snow-melt waters roar down the mountain.

The joy cry of virility stirs quivers:
from your navel I bite the ivory flower.
Bud-firm, you have opened under thunder,
in your galleries my shapeless flame would dwell.
So I shall soothe your tender wound,
the one that's life-long, and unhealable.

1967

87

Night ferry

Origins – they are dim in time, colossally
locked in the terrible mountain, buried in seaslime,
or vapourized, being volatile. What purpose
has the traveller now, whose connection is cut
with the whale, the wolf or the albatross? What does your small
        mouth
tell of supernovas or of chromosomes?
There are ivory graveyards in jungled valleys,
rainbow treasures, harps that sing in the wind,
fabled wrecks where the dead sailors sleep and a cuttlefish
sleeps on a bed of old doubloons.
                              Black bows
cleave water, suffer the waves. Finding the wet
deck, funnels, covered cargo, lifeboats
roped mute above the seasurge, pit-pat beats
the heart against the rail:
my flesh of salt clings to its molecules.

Oily and endless the stream is a truth drug. Pick
up signals from vast space, gather a ghoulish cry
from an astronaut lost for ever, his electronic
panels blipping with danger signs. Below
crushed like the foil on a Cracker Barrel cheese pack
a nuclear submarine no longer muscles
into the thunderous pressure. Is it the infinite
sound I hear that's going where? and to
whom can the intelligence be given? who are you?
Not only this, but also
between us the sensory network registers
potential tones, imaginable patterns
for there are destinies as well as destinations.

Screw churns through the superstructured
centuries of shut night, washing waters:
waves dip away, swell back, break open
in froth swaths and moon cobbles.

A snatch of Bach that intervenes
fluently pours through the portholes of my ears.
Boat on the Irish waters though I hear
poignant voices, whisper of snow, spring forests.
That set up plangencies, and issue oddthoughts.
With the ephemeral melody transistored.
Your eyes also seem to feature.

O are you daylight, love, to diminish my mist?
Siren, or the breeze's child, forgetful
while reaching through my bones?
In rest rooms people crowd, sleeping fug-
postured. Anyway of whom do I think?

I find an empty bunk, bend
under the muffled light, lie
in half-sleep, knock knock goes
the who's there night — a to-fro bottle tinkles.
It is the seasway, wavespeak, dance of angles.
Listen and you listen. Those are bilge-pipes.
Some are nightsounds, far from bird cries. Or a shark's snore.
The radius of consciousness is infinite, but seesaws.

Obscene are the unborn children, insane are the destitute mothers,
I do not think, who have known them, disowned them.
The contours of cowdung, or snow in the cold hills
criss-crossing earthwards, or zigzag catgut
stitches on chest incisions — these are the merely
straightline rhythms, level planes, the simplicity ratio.
Then there's you
who must somewhere exist to be regarded
as needy, needed, night-bound: a cherished enigma.

1967

Waiting

The isolation of exile is a gutted
warehouse at the back of pleasure streets:
the waterfront of limbo stretches panoramically —
night the beautifier lets the lights
dance across the wharf.
I peer through the skull's black windows
wondering what can credibly save me.
The poem trails across the ruined wall
a solitary snail, or phosphorescently
swims into vision like a fish
through a hole in the mind's foundation, acute
as a glittering nerve.

Origins trouble the voyager much, those roots
that have sipped the waters of another continent.
Africa is gigantic, one cannot begin
to know even the strange behaviour furthest
south in my xenophobic department.
Come back, come back mayibuye
cried the breakers of stone and cried the crowds
cried Mr. Kumalo before the withering fire
mayibuye Afrika

Now there is the loneliness of lost
beauties at Cabo de Esperancia, Table Mountain:
all the dead poets who sang of spring's
miraculous recrudescence in the sandscapes of Karoo
sang of thoughts that pierced like arrows, spoke
through the strangled throat of multi-humanity
bruised like a python in the maggot-fattening sun.

You with your face of pain, your touch of gaiety,
with eyes that could distil me any instant
have passed into some diary, some dead journal
now that the computer, the mechanical notion
obliterates sincerities.

The amplitude of sentiment has brought me no nearer
to anything affectionate,
new magnitude of thought has but betrayed
the lustre of your eyes.

You yourself have vacated the violent arena
for a northern life of semi-snow
under the Distant Early Warning System:
I suffer the radiation burns of silence.
It is not cosmic immensity or catastrophe
that terrifies me:
it is solitude that mutilates,
the night bulb that reveals ash on my sleeve.

1967

Immigrant

Don't travel beyond
Acton at noon in the intimate summer light
of England

to Tuskaloosa, Medicine Hat, preparing
for flight

dismissing the blond aura of the past
at Durban or Johannesburg
no more chewing roots or brewing riots

Bitter costs exorbitantly at London
airport in the neon heat
waiting for the gates to open

Big boy breaking out of the masturbatory
era goes
like eros over atlantis (sunk
in the time-repeating seas, admire our
tenacity)
jetting into the bulldozer civilization
of Fraser and Mackenzie
which is the furthest west that man has gone

A maple leaf is in my pocket.
X-rayed, doctored at Immigration
weighed in at the Embassy
measured as to passport, smallpox, visa
at last the efficient official informs me
I am an acceptable soldier of fortune, don't

tell the Commissioner
I have Oxford poetry in the satchel
propped between my army surplus boots
for as I consider Western Arrow's
pumpkin pancake buttered peas and chicken canadian style

in my mind's customs office
questions fester that turn the menu
into a visceral whirlpool. You can see
that sick bags are supplied.

Out portholes beyond the invisible propellers
snow mantles the ground peaks over Greenland.
What ice island of the heart has weaned
you away from the known white kingdom
first encountered at Giant's Castle?
You walked through the proteas nooked in the sun rocks
I approached you under the silver trees.
I was cauterized in the granite glare
on the slopes of Table Mountain, I was baffled
by the gold dumps of the vast Witwatersrand
when you dredged me from the sea like a recent fossil.

Where are the mineworkers, the compound Africans,
your Zulu ancestors, where are
the root-eating, bead-charmed Bushmen, the Hottentot sufferers?
Where are the governors and sailors of the
Dutch East India Company, where are
Eva and the women who laboured in the castle?
You are required as an explanation.

Glaciers sprawl in their jagged valleys,
cool in the heights, there are mountains and mountains.
My prairie beloved, you whose eyes are
less forgetful, whose fingers are less oblivious
must write out chits for the physiotherapy customers
must fill out forms for federal tax.

Consolatory, the air whiskies my veins.
The metal engines beetle on to further destinations.
Pilot's voice reports over Saskatchewan
the safety of this route, the use of exits,

facility of gas masks, Western Arrow's
miraculous record. The flat sea washes
in Vancouver bay. As we taxi in
I find I can read the road signs.

Maybe she is like you, maybe most women
deeply resemble you, all of them are
all things to all poets: the cigarette girl
in velvet with mink nipples, fishnet thighs,
whose womb is full of tobacco.
Have a B.C. apple in the A.D. city of the saviour,
and sing the centennial song.

1967

Rationale

I

So many voices that I speak with into
the white oblivion of escape
bounce blank against the TV opera
or battling for gravity and scope contend
with ghosts and snow or a statement of static:

yet will it suddenly crystallize,
the banal breath glow with kernels . . .
memorably so, though at the crux of love
labour of a postman introduces the humdrum
or body guards wrestle with the shocked assassin.

Propelled by the blandishments of the media
vulture photographers record the cortege;
flash news strikes root while my carnal fictions
haze on dead ceilings and fructify
nowhere near the global focus.

The pall of existence smoothly dissolves
in passive deceptions, passive receptions:
the periscope of the listener's eye
is misted by the spittle of the ocean.

II

Riding the cross swells I hang loose
past circling fins. The dolphin song
brings me ashore on lotus islands long
ravaged by lizard and weed. Lesbos is lost
and decapitated Orpheus bloats in the swell of the gulf
rocked in the water swirl and in the gullies
where Sappho and the nymphs had danced:
bones of the mad women torture my sinews

who hope to convey them to burial
through the forest of Venus fly-traps
that flower in mouths whose lips function.

Beauty, spiked with wonder, is the lure
for these my threnodies. Consider that
skinless teeth of the past are not
to be read as insinuendoes:
'This way all that is mortal goes'.
However laughter is admissible and
welcome indeed
words scatalogically smashing their way through the web of flushers
with the wind in the dry grass benignly stirring the turds.

March 1968

Hope hotel

Dawn light over my hotel notepaper
with a bird's alert incursion breaks
in softly potent rhythms to the simple provocation
of rain's splashy dissonance at windows.

Wet threads against the blue glass gleam:
this street that will be full of honeymoney soon
awaits today's invasions as I exorcise
the stigma of my own inexactitudes.

In a book of nudes the tortoise of the mind
feeds in isolation, and against the flesh horizons
of curvaceous models, voluptuous stone,
thinly stand those pyramids, hang those gardens

through which meanders the river bringing
pesticides from upland farms, the effluence of our lifeblood.
The rain-forest now still breathes though
the chimneys of the pulp mills belch sulphur.

Depressed confessions come through normal channels
with the word-order wishing not to change
as I watch the river and the snow runnels
where the fire sun will melt the wounds of winter.

The lush woods luminesce in green explosions
and the rich valleys regiment with ease
my scope, confined my art: it is not worth
consideration even now to win back selfhood.

British Colombia, 1968

Freedom

The heart is a stone in water.
Stone pulse up through the swell.
It seldom manages to aid loneliness.
There is no man left alive now.

Perhaps in this sense, this poem:
I am sorry, I said.
Put a little love in your free soul, listen.
It becomes itself, it does,
not being what but how.

The gods pounded in my ear,
and the devil stood laughing at my elbow.

I drank vodka urgently.
In the fireplace I started,
at a dead summer, dust on brickwork.

Toronto, August 1969

Quiet desperation

Not here blows
the south wind open through the field,
no black twigs tremble in the rain
or the earth laugh.
You are under Hydro's power.

Snow spins as Christmas comes.
Ripples of the coarse grass over old graves,
lashing of the water against eaten
pocked pocked and bitterwashed
sea-wall
       doesn't lyrically sad
                    reach my ears, pervade
    my eyes.

No spume washes on the river stones
my bronze women
       youthed in chains but —
fleshed artlessly
through the eye's senses;
       only the drought of masspapers,
       motor din and gasoline clang that knot my nerves,
       sulphur miasma, neon, give me soda
       waiter who also serves.

Blind with fumes you stare at
Simpson's store directory:
five washrooms are for women, two for men.
With such trivia intriguing yourself,
chill winter as you pick your way
past the warehouse, the Eaton's sale (Jumbo).

My mind hurts with consistent
intake of chemicals:
Slim-mint sabbaths, long walks in the dog park,
librium for angst Mondays,

diet foods for I have drunk
much beer, flung suds
down my gullet, largely
the brown bottle looms in dishevelment
in my room of kisses and cold sleep.
    Crumbs on the dog-eared novels
    in this city whose
    rotten bonanza I earn.

Toronto, Winter 1970

Return to the city of the heart

Hardly worthwhile the time lacuna
elsewhere in monied metropoli
near to north pole, thought as I
emptied the aftershave down my spine
and patted hand lotion on my navel
jetting east over Ireland
and smelling nice over Cornwall,
landing on a London Saturday.

At Bird In Hand the dollars are
happily misunderstood
because in making that waste motion
the ache of sanity's assuaged,
years of rat's sleep in my room
troubled by the seven devils
are at an ocean's remove.
Sinews of melancholy
tug at their bollards, but
now with a throatsong deep and drinknight long
you and I unite with these islands.

My life now cruxes in the old
                    solidities:
going by the river up to eros.
The air is brickfield wet.
Wintering howsome the roots grip
                stone soil
or glad seed sleep
            in any earth.
It is March: am I averse?
                No I do not
                yet say
        falling on my feet
        with some of the nine lives

left in my bag of flesh.
Far from my native town and soil
it is out of the blue
nostalgia that I land tranquil.
Toward this world having come
after all is an achievement.

Predictably engaged
                again I am
amaranth in one bed
                beautiful body of Christ in another.
The prince of taxi riders may however
meet anytime the face that is appealing
high up in a red bus, a pub, a club
perhaps disguised
                as a cool drunk, Afro—Saxon bred
winsome intellectual (ex
Dark Continent-congratulate me here)
                or dozy in the double bed
                somewhat maladroit at making music.
All is forgiven though,
of elsewhere this is untrue even if
I walk with an address book
full of crossed-out numbers, party contacts,
once-met twice-kissed women who have moved
to somewhere I will never be, black pepper
desired more than someone else's allspice.

                Despite the irony, she, city,
                suckled my exile:
        I am back
with a bagful bonanza of travellers' cheques,
wishing not to appear soulsick, washed-up, blackmailed, whitewashed

                perhaps a little footsore and war-weary,
but just now free in the street
                                        after abortive America
availably labile
supportably poetic

London, March 1970

Dogsbody half-breed

I

The magnet of exotica that draws
sailors from their holds, blood from the sword,
is that which elicits a gravid sigh
(as witness Captain Cook or sullen Bligh),
is that which brought blond settlers like a hex
into the heartland, oxdrawn, ammunitioned.
Over the rocks, through drought, the laager treks
by fire out of stone, by daycloud holy,
unto a covenant against the Zulu.

Once this was Tormentoso, Cape of Storms,
midway station for the scurvied crews,
bordello for the sea-tossed Dutchman, cum
point d'appui for the growers of wine
beyond whose vineyards stretched the purlieus
of Governor van der Stel in time
before there was an overland
expansion into farm and mine.
Maternal muscle of my mixed-blood life
with child were you heavy, with discontent rife.

II

Some are tanned by the sun and some
sweat satined in a slum concealment:
white beach or pismire ghetto, through factotum
eyes I am aware of, having spent
at the annealing tunnel, the conveyor belt,
the last ounce of energy for the master of my salt.

Yet glittering with tears I see you pass
in armoured cars, divided from yourself
by golden fortune, natural largesse,
forgetting quite in the siren or the bell

pealing your sanctity, wailing a daily violence,
your bastardies, abortions, sins of silence,
those marooned, dragooned, those massacred or shackled
by your few chosen from the many called.

III

Bitter though the taste be, it is life somehow.
Despite the dark night of long ago, in spring now
looking from Lion's Head or Devil's Peak,
your delicate nooks and moments noble-gentle
bud-open both to blond and black
and I hybrid, after Mendel,
growing between the wire and the wall,
being dogsbody, being me, buffer you still.

Balsam Street, Toronto, April 1970

Be at

be at
where
the younghard here-and-now.
and sometimes too
strident voices
sing together
                of love, though
some might not hear these veiled rhapsodies
and the Wall Street heathen might shudder
                I listen as
part of that sweet and sour body
world united
there are
guitars and drums and orchestras and east
instruments.
                in mixed groups making
country folk and rock music
the stone blue blowers
and the bedrock swingers

a little good
will come from this
                whether the light or heavy
                permeates the seventies, and so
be it.

April 1970

Words

```
        words
        from
        deep
        down

        come
        up
        slowly

        to
        a
        thin
        man
inside a fat poem
        wan-
        ting
        out
```

April 1970

Asseverations

The fire will not ask me to make its bed,
nor is there more than one room in the womb:
cold stone stands above you or instead
your ashes have been scattered in the wind.

Drops of compassion in the oceans of
humanity are bitterly invisible:
the rice-field and the rose-garden must blend
before the hand that sowed can waft in harvest.

Words I plant in this cool adversity
germinate in April ardour, green
fused push through sleep mist that has haunted (blanketed)*
the rich black soil of midnight in the brain,

I ghost-wrote tales in Africa, pseudonymous and,
hunched in shack or hovel in pursuit
of truths in rhythms, nocturnes, melodies:
grappled with the hardship of a rhyme.

The liberators are unnameable,
with winter in their hair perhaps, themselves
hexed, or fallen in the rape of grass,
whose recipes are now illegible.

Out of such haze, such loss, the luck of birth,
must be fashioned never questionably
strength of seed and courage of decision.
There is never work without resistance.

April 1970

* *Presumably Nortje had second thoughts about which word to use,
but never made a final choice.*

Shock therapy

Madness is evident when you want to
dream of nothing, laid in hard
fastnesses of amber, be the marble
gilt forever in the glass facade.

Dementia claws at he who of a sudden
rips away the cloud that filters no
manna through his veins, speech through his tongue:
stabs time, that robber baron, in the torso.

Frantic the violater of the unities:
his day and night are of no consequence;
such drama takes the shape of motion
anywhere, at anyone's expense.

Nor does the nihilist live less dangerously
though caught in the hysteria of silence:
loathe to wake to the light he may lie
wombed in warmth, with knees up to the chin.

Spreadeagled in the blue gore on the page
or tightening the words to pearls of sweat
that the busy brain fosters from a latent life,
shock is the stilling therapy for the poet.

Toronto, April 1970

Poem

Become to me a sweet song
as before said I
        stone in water mute
the day burglar of booze
steals into these defiances of un-
silent lucubrations

The world in unpeace manufactures
jets, bazookas, books of strategy
flamethrow napalm or barrage
        the ports of learning, so
with black hands I write
by a fire with a big log that unsplit
        won't incinerate
though the small flames lick tenaciously
from a bed of orange, doctored coals.

What journals of the exile yesterdays
will be carboned in that grate
when the snow forecast
for the afternoon arrives.

Become to me as black
as my hands
        with the soot of memory
expunged
        as in the rose dusk or morninggold
        my love
        my now distant land

Toronto, April 1970

Leftovers

with buttermilk sky covering space
and beauty of the countries south
gestapoed into disbelief
    we who have tarzaned, o my brothers,
will find the air aciduous
the muse expired

the senses whimper in these brutal times
    should the tongue not shrill its bitterness:
      I now may have to trust my nose
into the arctic of the telephone
    follow the braille
                of a roughcast wall
into a livingroom beyond
            the odour of sleep
            and stench of dreams
which pay out phobias
            obsessions
                guilts
    in lump sums making waking lip
a paranoidal nightmare among snarled cars, profit commerce, t.v.
messages between the shootings
    and further escalations
    (follow them to China if you must)
I must
    clear my ears of wax congestion
while speaking through the hole in the wall of my mind
    where the wreckers' ball pounds
            merciless pendulum:
puffs of dust
bloom from my mouth
            and arid are
these talcumed valleys where
        hair, now musty

smelt fragrant

April 1970

Nightly

My heart is not at all in this word ritual
because I've peered into dark doorways
and with shoulders hunched seen the ceiling change shape,
sat trembling with a mind that is polluted:
squeezed out images like pips
from a stale orange
while glancing at the drawn curtains nervously:
in the end strung together a cheap necklace
trying to buy off my inquisitors.

I have felt my loins go numb at the blue burn of alcohol
touching the tinder of the grief-shattered guts
and my pulse jump fifty feet at the sound in the cellar,
the tentacles of resting hands recoil and the clenched teeth
hold back a scream of terror in the ghost-infested midnight
when there is only space and me.

The clock is torture, Torquemada
equipped with an electric whip
plugged into this ageing century:
the rack has gone the way of the pterodactyl
but the freezer that stops pumping through its circuit
resumes startingly quite at random:
this is the horror of insomnia
that makes me decline
caffeine stimulation
in favour of an anodyne.

Here come the Job afflictions that
reduce the man to ash:
it is almost sabotage to fash-
ion thought into a moody architecture,
in the small hours push
a probe through the pus into wounded flesh,
through the scalded membrane or the soul blister,
feel for the trauma, expel the black-toothed beast

112

there entrenched, hacking at the fibre,
or the thirteen satans strumming on my lifeline
mutinous dissonances.

The senses atrophy though I have long been
discharged from the colony of lepers;
I have lived on benzedrine
attempting to get a paper
                sedulously, by a flickering candle
                a smoky lamp in a black township
that would get me through the wall.

Though the broken buds can heal and even blossom
again at some auspicious time,
the rise and fall of blood believe me
can trouble almost anybody given
the hour and the place. I breathe a heavy
sigh of human regard and own relief
at dawn when the devils flee their stations
and birds start to wake the universe.

Toronto, April 1970

Poem: South African

       and at last then the nostalgia
palliates itself
so I can rise
          midmorningmute
and sing through its shroud
having looked
           on shattered faces dark with terror
                  drugged with clouded sunshine
come from
       scarred landscapes
       earth
       raped
          goldrich once the world was
          far away
              for me in my home rain
          which grew rainbows
now love is long
          distanced in
   a telephone call
and passengers
          crowd the ports
bound out
       by sea and air
and land
the wind guillotines
          your correspondences
but these broken sentences
    stumble to heaven on the hill despite
    the man with the whip who beats my
    emaciated words back

they die but
       at last
get us all together as a vision
    incontrovertible, take me as evidence

Toronto, April 1970

Nightfall

The black trunks holding up their canopies
are hushed at dusk. Tattered, the green drapes **stir**
as skies darken in between and heaven has
no more candles for tonight. Up there

thunder spoke a summer sermon
but watery and little was the soothing rain,
and now I cannot even see the common
clouds because I'm waiting for the sun.

Wishy-washy are the sweet tomorrows
and most amazing our tenacious hopes:
the cat sleeps in the corner as I throw
cold water on these unromantic notes.

Toronto, May 1970

Poem in Toronto

Eternal curtains drape this loft
with lilac walls around me.
A view towards the beech-tree landscape
swirls with blossoms and the throbbing sun
in middle May, the lakeshore waters rich
with the poison tide of phosphates feeding algae,
feeding the killing weeds
from the bilge of a million
miraculous machines.

Lying prone with the dormant seed of syphilis
lodger in my skull
and a whisky feeling coming through the sky
I hear the world at work
busy doing this that and the other,
and make of sleep a saviour.

Somewhat reluctant now the night
will fall upon my doorknob
and it may rain with glints of tears
against the windowpanes
while my words spew through the sewers
in the company of beer cans, bob among
plastic flotsam, long-lived soapsuds, garbage of
the good city,
as rising for a token show of life
when the heart sits like a rock in the throat,
unemployable in that regard,
I watch a TV movie, hold some commerce
with Speedy the cat perhaps or with a waning cigarette.

May 1970

116

Native's letter

Habitable planets are unknown or too
far away from us to be
of consequence. To be of
value to his homeland must the wanderer
not weep by northern waters, but love
his own bitter clay
roaming through the hard cities, tough
himself as coffin nails.

Harping on the nettles of his melancholy,
keening on the blue strings of the blood,
he will delve into mythologies perhaps
call up spirits through the night.

Or carry memories apocryphal
of Tshaka, Hendrik, Witbooi, Adam Kok,
of the Xhosa nation's dream
as he moonlights in another country:

but he shall also have
cycles of history
outnumbering the guns of supremacy.

Now and wherever he arrives
extending feelers into foreign scenes
exploring times and lives,
equally may he stand and laugh,
explode with a paper bag of poems,
burst upon a million televisions
with a face as in a Karsh photograph,
slave voluntarily in some siberia
to earn the salt of victory.

Darksome, whoever dies
in the malaise of my dear land
remember me at swim,

the moving waters spilling through my eyes:
and let no amnesia
attack at fire hour:
for some of us must storm the castles
some define the happening.

Toronto, May 1970

A house on Roncesvalles, Toronto 222

hesitant about whether
to fetch out pen and paper
I wonder will thought dribble
while the radiator weeps into its coils
           (or will profundities escape
              before I can scan the news and
              the man who pays for it comes home
              at 8 o'clock)

windowpane ice-cold to my survey
saving my fingertips I test with my knuckles
which is what a corpse under the first
snowfall has no earthly need to do
           (I the living take account
              of anatomy and function:
              runnels from the nose
              find a shallow grave in Kleenex: seems
              the flesh which breeds it cannot cope;
              in bedrooms likewise drips
              honey resin from the taut torso;
              through the root seep
              tonic juices,
              the groin sweats under talc
              in the bathroom where
              I sneeze and relish
              the warm coils of the soul's home realizations)

city leaves in late October
when the blood and gold tones of autumn
cower under crowns of white
and this itself is wonderful remembering
smokestacks belching fumes in a wasteland
of freight trains and beef factories
           (how should one forget
              the dew of April, swans on the pond, ambrosial sunshine

an hour in the library and winter
deferred to this tea-bag half-light,
a season of nail-end faith)

a secular poem will note
unpalatable truths:
city of judges with Kapuskasing faces
(there I've never been by autombile),
wine addicts in the park who bum nickels;
one scarred spatula cheekboned Indian owned
an old Ford with the dust of summer caking
the corruption of them both.

I am he who
let the ornaments fade
because of the dog days that were upon us
because of the walk in the moondust which they made
a marvel more than snow on the mute boughs.
            (these are not the respecters of trees
                who burdened us with plastic bags of rocks
                to plant in planetariums)
under the grime and slime the heart beats non-stop
apple strong

Toronto, May 1970

Notes from the middle of the night

I

Untold anxieties through the dark
cannot at random exorcise themselves
it is me, black, menaced among the shelves:
of books and intellectual rubble,
who loves the both-end candle life with benzedrine
and must answer to the seven devils.
A world of memories swirls
and the gallstones of fear jab at my shredded nerves.

Inside me blooms a sudden wish
to calm fright with a little yellow pill,
lullaby it to a predawn slumber,
escape by soporific in an orange capsule.
There blows a flowering death release
in winds from Lethe, Styx or anywhere
forgetfulness resides.

II

Through the flow of silence, tenor of night,
unlovely the butterfly guts that won't relax
the brain that reeks with guilt feelings
hearing a peripatetic devil
in the cooling of a floorboard or a cat's tread
demoniacal laughter in a dog's bark
instant sorrow of an icebox starting up
the cold motor jerking juice for its circuit
out of my bloodstream, freezing me to the spot.

Malodorous beads of sweat on a dull brow
are wafted dry by the first bird's song:
in the streetlight twinkle through the screen of trees
discern the sanity seeping back along

disordered channels, but undoubtedly
further torture awaits whoever is
speedtrapped in the nets and webs of timespace.

III

With grey light comes another breathing spell:
I assemble words that bittersweetly sing
along the axis of the golden star.
I will lay me down to sleep in strong sunshine
airing these fretful sentiments,
with a sigh letting go these obsessions.

The city can manage its population of rats
ferociously baring their fangs for the sake of a dollar
while I have not a thimbleful's desire
to avail myself of the barbed-wire era's afflatus
or espouse the puritan virtues that never mature
and profit only the pork-barrel people.

Toronto, May 1970

Seen one, take one

The professional guns are out in jungle fatigues,
picking their way round dung-tipped bamboo spikes,
sensing movement in the world of leaves.
I read their trigger fingers, minds efflorescing
to poisonous intent. The sergeant almost
bursts at the joints with tension as he tightens
his true-blue shoulders in a recoilless moment:
but Charlie-baby is wily with patience,
fed on a diet of rice and General Giap's
'One cannot love the enemy unless
he is near enough to touch.'

Leaves waft. Rain is suggested. Insects
in vague clouds settle on the festered swamp.
The tiger stalks in black pyjamas
thin and starved, his lean jaws
stuck in a brotherly rictus
to the sallow blade of his nose the sparse valley of his mouth
the disconsolate planets of eyes.

'Tiger, tiger' – this is how
an English correspondent used to wire
his story from Saigon, until a Paris
newsman from a chopper up in Hue
startled the Frogs over their breakfast with
'Who is Charlie? What is he?'
which made a Russian politician say
in Pravda:
'Bland as an icicle he hangs in a heaven of flamethrowers.
Reaction is chemical, death is mechanical,
they teach you at the School of Instant Pictures.

You should see me shooting the scene with hot lead flying:
the most fearless photographer yet.
Communication, that's the message
my editor goes for – a marvellous shot

of a V.C. skinned by Koreans, strung from a tree,
or a multi-exposure of a human wave
attack at dawn requiring extra film.
At the moment though the combat zone
is dead as a coffin lid.

The ominous quiet only makes me think
of past life, the divorce in Acapulco
last time I was home between
Korea and Vietnam. I couldn't really
expect you to be lonely, and I only
wanted to be free — as we say here
'Seen one, Take one', which is why
America can never be the same again.
I'm going with the first plane to Cambodia.

May 1970

Reflections in a passing mirror

In the deepsea reaches you can not
get near China or call Peru:
nothing except
remember Pericles, perhaps
view an albatross
sight a blue whale.

In the constipated crust of earth
you may with difficulty
dig up Etruscan artifacts, translate
the stones of ages past,
piece together with a scalpel
mammoth bones.

The ionosphere is riddled with
atoms of electric and a hairline
fracture can be fatal to
passengers of the sky.
You can not tell precisely when
the sun will blow its fuse.

Now beautiful is the love thing
sweet the word
peace to a thousand understandings:
the trumpeter swan in danger of extinction
is like the lizard of Komodo
saved, while our wars
go on.

In a discotheque
I feed on snacks, drinks:
cacophony transmogrified to me
becomes a grotto silence, murk
this music, strobe greens, purples
and the spinning wheels of night, neoned outside
with the glare that flares between
the living and the dead.

Tearsweat, smoke, and sentiment,
blood coursing over drowned islands
where once the heart was beached.
Again I have not washed, I smell,
but why blush in the dark of life
when this booze breath is ripe
and words nullifying?
No sin against the world
can be committed by a heartbeat.

Because the brow burns
and the nostrils quiver
and the loins hunger or scream rape
sometimes
I never
forget in the middle
of nothing but a love ache every day
the gifted past, unspoilable.

May 1970

Poem (for?)

through all these changes in the air
and the night electrified by green explosions,
blue of the haze and the hangover fug
(morning in the room without a lock
when grey
fear persists
with an irrationality become impossible)
your limbs live like branches of the sun

and I remember Arcady
paradise of roses, magic clouds and thunderbolts
as we shoot the bull,
that fake animal, bloodless
              (I on edge of bathtub watching you
              wash the years
              out of your eyes)
the laughter rings
my love, my keeper

London, August 1970

'The drifting seeds of summer . . .'

The drifting seeds of summer ply backyard gardens
over walls and weaving shadows:
mended now, the muscles catch
sights of the falling sunshine, light that
spills through windows, leaves
            shining in the blue air.
That bird sings, eloquent and seemly
in daybursts, calling
calling with a sweet clarity, contrapuntally against the roar of traffic
        trucksour [*ms illegible*]

Now as it happens
among the trees and the restored
houses,
walking into the Boston Arms,
tripping off the cobbles and into the adequate atmosphere
noon flows like calm over these London suburbs.
Here I stand in the most
beautiful of revivals, freshened into
lovesong tenderness, cool and lyrical
with no halfway feelings, no
dryness in the throat, because
I breathe you.

London, August 1970

Untitled

That that is lost and found again
seldom is as beautiful. Some lustre
rubbed off in the night amid the neon
usage. Some sound deadened in a dark chair.

You are saddened looking in a pawnshop:
in a dusty window, faded, and stained
see knick-knacks, gilt lamps, second-hand stock.
Some come to buy, some reluctantly refrain.

Few come to redeem from the miscellany. These
items may be wanted but the wherewithal
is lacking. You sit and read obituaries,
visit a barbershop, walk around in a fruitstall. .

London, September 1970

Sonnet (love of perversity)

Love of perversity, rage and vice,
unknown to all who live complacently,
drive me to lunacy, compel confessions
I am loathe to make were I at Peter's Gate.

There would I lurch in drunkenness and hate,
committing torturous blasphemies
as now I loaf among the well-to-do
and not among the louts and down-and-outers, tramps.

Could I but flay the skins of gentleman
tough-minded, soft-spoken, delicate, well-heeled,
responsible for systems that have bred
oil tycoons, bankers, men in real estate!
Businessmen and beggars are equally fraudulent.
One can see marvels in devil's excrement.

London, September 1970

Nasser is dead

Are not the Arabs cousins of the Jews?
Millions pour into Cairo
whose grief is inconsolable.
No-one
can stem the spread of fire or the flow of tears.

I think of the sons of Africa sometimes
and my heart bursts.
When I think of Chaka or Christ the rebel
my heart bursts.

The Queen of Sheba came from the south.
Solomon, they say, was wise. David was strong, killed giants.
I have heard of Cleopatra proving
very wily, very
beautiful. And my heart bursts.

Hulks of ships clog Suez,
sandbagged bunkers on either side.
The Red Sea ports are closed.
Jordan cannot be crossed,
the Syrians are punished for their impunity.
Palestine with its ragged refugees
is won or lost, depending on who speaks the word
through the barrel of whose gun.
They are still fighting in Amman.
At the Wailing Wall they have stopped
knocking their heads against the stone, a
brief respite.

Farouk ails in Switzerland.
Is he not dead? I do not know.
So much has happened since the Ptolemies reigned
and the British marshals and generals withdrew.
One may say that Napoleon

departed in haste, there are readings and schools
of history, someone translated the Rosetta Stone-hieroglyphics,
and the Sahara is timeless.

So much water has drained from the heartland lakes
and yet they never dry up.
So much has happened between Khufu, between Cheops
and the liberation of the fellahin. All over Africa marched the ravagers,
Alexandria burnt and flames ate the pages of books.

But are not the Arabs cousins of the Jews?
Aswan, that great work,
was almost broken by the raiders.
Abu Simbel was first saved piece by piece: I understand
it cost the Americans millions.

One wonders who
plundered the Pyramids, found the tunnels.
No worse than a bank
robbery, stealing the mummies.

Some of the monstrous blocks have fallen
claimed by the desert.
And all over Africa the gourds are broken,
the calabashes empty at one time or another.
Spears are buried or removed
but don't we all eat with knives?
We cannot be converted in a decade.
Boots litter Gaza. The carnage ebbs and flows.
Rusting tanks are the last monuments.
Millions mourn a train longer than the Nile:
their flood of tears cannot be beaten back,
and the rich silt is the salt on women's cheeks,
sweat on the brows of men.

London, September 1970

132

Sonnet one

Supremely individual, flamboyant, proud,
insane and thirsty for a stable life,
attacked by love's dementia, and predicaments and loud
laughter at the skyjackings, world troubles and world strife,

in cosmopolitan dives of some metropolis
I know that this is not the universe,
and how the rain shines through the sun and stars
explode within a galaxy remains mysterious.

The poisoned spring has bubbled through my veins:
Young Venus lay in rags I loved her so –
Dog of ferocity. The golden road turned blue
becomes a damp and rampant thoroughfare for sins
of carnality, of turpitude. The smelly and the raw
crowds that disgust me are also those I adore.

London, September 1970

Sonnet two

I have drunk up nights and spent the days
in wild pursuits, life of the libertine:
do not repent, confess, seek remedies.
The bourgeois sinners are banned from where I've been.

The desperate either go mad with self-disgust
or steal or rob from the immaculate:
through sheer loathing some have stood and passed
water against the walls. Expectorate

politely in your chamber pots. I speak
to you for whom spittoons are made, who buy
furbelows and leopard skins, antiques.
Will you not read it, this my poetry,
calling it uncouth: it makes you sick?
You serve your tea in china that's authentic.

London, September 1970

134

Sonnet three

What is mundane I wish to make sublime.
What ordinarily moves upon the ground
can rise and rainbow, shooting from the slime,
can glow in revelation, can transcend.

I have tasted potables, edibles, all that flesh
can offer: lain in luxury with rich women,
and homosexuals, bums, rag-pickers so obsessed
me I could watch them all for hours in fascination.

Unpalatable beast, or you who think
I revel in disgust, yourself are cloyed
with chocolates and caviar, discreetly stink;
in self-indulgence, secret self-abuse
you wallow in self-same mud, know not the void
I as a sycophant wander in, timeserver to the Muse.

London, September 1970

Jazz trio

Through my pernod glaze musicians
drum absorbedly, cello their phrases, riff
on old pianos the bald melodies.

Through the empty kettle spring tensions,
over the top of a glass fingers that shift
smell of beer and rapidly punish the ivories.

Interval tunes sprout out of a jukebox for sixpence,
then the snaredrums rimshots develop a surprise
oasis of warmth. At the window are some eyes
looking in like stones. There's paltry sense
in jazz without the intimacies inside
a cloudy room where fervour grows towards
a session's end; at closing time who can hide
Bach or Beethoven from the improving bards?

London, September 1970

Natural sinner

I have preyed on my emotions like a mantis,
have lain with Soho prostitutes and gambled
a month's rent in machines that gobble sixpences,
and have sufficiently recovered from the shambles

to tell not belletristically but
in measured music of a sort, in tones
more harsh than soothing, how the glut
of worms in meat has forced verse from my bones.

For your sake who have sometimes those reverses
suffered that the hobo has or tramp
walking through a Job's rain of curses,
invisible has become I hope the stamp
of birth, of blackness, criminality:
I speak this from experience, speak from me.

London, September 1970

137

Questions and answers

The underbelly of the shark shows when
song stops
and the reed that harped the wind
snaps.
Which Dutch Reformed Churchman has the sheer gall
not to compensate the looted Kaffir?
I asked at the golden portals
and no-one answered me, not one.
I asked at the broken gates.

After war, after poverty

After war, after poverty
we have become effigies, camera pabulum,
ineffectual scarecrows guarding the corn.
            And the dead point their fingers at some growing girl:
            she shall have tin cans slung from her shoulders,
            she shall have leaden balls on her toes.
We are caught
in colourful postures at shanty entrances
with corrugated faces trapped in Kodacolor.
The Information Bureau do not tell you who
is sweeping Parliament floors after the great
incomprehensible debates of the Potchefstroom Doctors:
the Bloemfontein farmers have more to say
about where I must live and work than
Adam Kok's descendants or Nelson Mandela the lawyer
who because of the golden words that sprang from his black mouth
languishes in a stone cage and may not even
try to swim the Hellespont to Cape Town.

I do not to salvation move

I have broken free of those excellent unctions
administered in the name of my country's honour.
I have rejected the domains of gold
because I was living with the burning devil:

138

(Apollo was martyred by the masters
and the keepers of the keys of the kingdom
made us eat husks and baboon flesh
while they drank the nectar)
Rimbaud's nightmares or the evil flowers
that sprout in the festering alleys of Johannesburg
proclaim the blackmass I will hold
(and who shall stop me, Charles Engelhard?)
I will not to salvation move
being transplanted from here to there
endorsed out to some alien native land
(Cape Town to Transkei on the night train:
Matanzima ruled there a land
of eroded paupers)
I will not slip across the border
patrolled by men with leashed Alsatians
snarling along the barbed wire fences
looking for a disturber of something or other:
I am no guerilla.
I will fall out of the sky as the Ministers gape from their front porch
and in broad daylight perpetrate atrocities
on the daughters of the boss:
ravish like Attila
and so acquire more scars myself
laughing as I infest the vulnerable liberals
with the lice inherited from their gold-mine fathers
(Cecil John Rhodes must not expect an apology
and I cannot but condole with Anton Rupert)
I have dug enough diamonds for them
in the blue pipes of Kimberley:
foreign crowns were studded with the stones of my sweat
(where is that piece of glass picked up by a Native
and christened the Cullinan Diamond?
They say it was expertly cut for Queen Victoria,
that imperious German lady)

There is none innocent

What are the 'thousands of innocents caught in the crossfire'
doing just standing there
on this vast battlefield
>   (British and American nationals I am afraid
>   cannot be evacuated from city hotels
>   where the fighting is fiercest: no Viscount, no Boeing 727, no
>   Red Cross mercy flight can land on one of those office blocks
>   47 storeys high, gilt edge investment).

Besides the scorpion that seldom stirs
has plenty of work to do:
>   (where is thy sting?)

Because the lion lies lazily now in the Kruger National Park
or only stalks the zoo
the hyena laughs:
>   (but for how long?)

I laugh myself to death that they should find
flesh no longer grass.
But forbiddingly we must issue a caveat to all the disinterested:
'This is not Biafra or Amman,
and the river cannot be crossed
once the tears are in spate.'

Exile from the first

Exile was implanted
in the first pangs of paradise. This land became
a refuge for adventurers.
And who remembers history
need not trouble my
head with tales. I underwent the fire
baptism, reared in rags, schooled
in the violence of the mud.

God's truth regardless of the death's rattle
(I come to execute what's pertinent)

or your stupendous array of guns
or the echelons of Stellenbosch cadets.
Effective immediately, stormtroopers
will be on recall from Rhodesian campaigns
and the Caprivi Strip will revert to peaceful marshland,
the base to keep watch on Zambia there
will be as much of a launching pad
as the rotting walls of Zimbabwe.
Those ramparts will break like so many reeds,
these towers tumble in a hail of stones.

For such were this Eldorado's
rife iniquities
that one would speculate
its hydra-headed births derive
from the malice of the sun
coupled with the boermeid's stern maternity:
white trash
coursing through my blood
for all the unalienable seasons,
and I have an incurable
malaise that makes me walk restlessly
through the sewers of these distant cities.

Who but to save me but myself?
I bred words in hosts, in vain, I'll have to
bleed: bleed for the broken mountains, lost
Umshlanga, Hangklip, Winterberg,
the starving rivers wait for me to plunge through
to the forefront,
the mud has hardened on my boots.
Ancestors will have their graves uprooted,
uncouth will be the interrogations and bloody the reprisals.

London, September 1970

Gratitude (to the British police)

To the just and those who serve the free
I bear my gratitude, unambiguous,
for fallen in Parliament Fields, remiss,
I could have done myself an injury.

Ouzo-drunk and lying in the road rootless,
bruised, obstinate inebriate, I cursed
for the seven devils those who tried to nurse
me, hack Samaritans, black-booted.

Sunday incarceration: it was mercy more
than the worst profligate or anarchist expects.
When the black bee buzzes in his golden cell
he is visited by the man in the shining armour;
those upon whom have been visited such punishments
can be grateful that the bullion priest condemns himself to hell.

London, September 1970

Bile and sympathy

Sifting these sonnets from the dreams that failed,
pitched at the numerous levels of reality,
I witness dread visions of grotesquerie,
romantic illusions to some mockeries nailed.

Adrenalin spurts through channels of fluorescence,
and green in a morning gullet leaps the bile.
Through the flowering mouth of Venus flies gall
blacker than the century's decadence.

Thus my Lazarus allusions and my Samson stance
present no Lambaréné boasts or shorn man the iconoclast,
and neither with the hives raided do I rifle all the symbolists
to translate new hells of similar circumstance.
September's ending scarcely embitters me.
Horror and love produce this melancholy.

London, September 1970

St Giles

A few graves
at the bicycle park
      Do I steal their soft dreams
      even now?

They, the dead, awaken
              no sorrow
     open
no fresh wound.

         Uncover in me no trauma:
I piss behind telephone booths
      watching stars, oh yes
it is me, my
     steam
     risin'

Oxford, October 1970

Reply to a correspondent, Olga

In those suburbs where the leaves cascade,
windswept by winter to which corners?
I, too fed on the glow of presences, made
log fires started with cardboard from the cellar.

And afterwards the pine was never bare
under the burden of snow. Music
reached it, though the bulbed tulips were frozen.
Out of our voices grew the unused

excellence of lifetimes. Dormant colours
crackled in the hearth, glowed in the grate's chinks.
Suns shone in the light of your labour,
so did a love I had long thought extinct.

So I idled my way through your house
under the blessing of the warm walls
and out of ordinary moods we sprang a taste
for late-night oysters, conversations,

discovery and revelation.
When the summer came we found we'd been so busy
tending fires and working on the inside
that an old acorn had grown into a tree.

One afternoon I left off television
and went to hack that stripling down.
It now occurs to me in the fall season
that I left the debris lying on the ground,

Oxford, October 1970

All hungers pass away

All hungers pass away,
we lose track of their dates:
desires arise like births,
reign for a time like potentates.

I lie and listen to the rain
hours before full dawn brings
forward a further day and winter sun
here in a land where rhythm fails.

Wanly I shake off sleep,
stare in the mirror with dream-puffed eyes:
I drag my shrunken corpulence
among the tables of rich libraries.

Fat hardened in the mouth,
famous viands tasted like ash:
the mornings-after of a sweet escape
ended over bangers and mash.

I gave those pleasures up,
the sherry circuit, arms of a bland girl
Drakensberg lies swathed in gloom,
starvation stalks the farms of the Transvaal.

What consolation comes
drops away in bitterness.
Blithe footfalls pass my door
as I recover from the wasted years.

The rain abates. Face-down
I lie, thin arms folded, half-aware
of skin that tightens over pelvis.
Pathetic, this, the dark posture.

Oxford, November 1970